FOREWORD

The collection of "Everything Will Be Okay" travel phrasebooks published by T&P Books is designed for people traveling abroad for tourism and business. The phrasebooks contain what matters most - the essentials for basic communication. This is an indispensable set of phrases to "survive" while abroad.

This phrasebook will help you in most cases where you need to ask something, get directions, find out how much something costs, etc. It can also resolve difficult communication situations where gestures just won't help.

This book contains a lot of phrases that have been grouped according to the most relevant topics. A separate section of the book also provides a small dictionary with more than 1,500 important and useful words.

Take "Everything Will Be Okay" phrasebook with you on the road and you'll have an irreplaceable traveling companion who will help you find your way out of any situation and teach you to not fear speaking with foreigners.

TABLE OF CONTENTS

T&P Books Publishing

T&P Books Publishing

PHRASEBOOK

— HEBREW —

THE MOST IMPORTANT PHRASES

This phrasebook contains
the most important
phrases and questions
for basic communication
Everything you need
to survive overseas

T&P BOOKS

By Andrey Taranov

Phrasebook + 1500-word dictionary

English-Hebrew phrasebook & concise dictionary

By Andrey Taranov

The collection of "Everything Will Be Okay" travel phrasebooks published by T&P Books is designed for people traveling abroad for tourism and business. The phrasebooks contain what matters most - the essentials for basic communication. This is an indispensable set of phrases to "survive" while abroad.

Another section of the book also provides a small dictionary with more than 1,500 useful words arranged alphabetically. The dictionary includes a lot of gastronomic terms and will be helpful when ordering food at a restaurant or buying groceries at the store.

T&P Books Publishing
www.tpbooks.com

ISBN: 978-1-78716-978-4

This book is also available in E-book formats.
Please visit www.tpbooks.com or the major online bookstores.

PRONUNCIATION

Letter's name	Letter	Hebrew example	T&P phonetic alphabet	English example
Alef	א	אריה	[ɑ], [ɑː]	bath, to pass
	א	אחד	[ɛ], [ɛː]	habit, bad
	א	מָאָה	['] (hamza)	glottal stop
Bet	ב	בית	[b]	baby, book
Gimel	ג	גמל	[g]	game, gold
Gimel+geresh	ג׳	ג׳ונגל	[dʒ]	joke, general
Dalet	ד	דג	[d]	day, doctor
Hei	ה	הר	[h]	home, have
Vav	ו	וסת	[v]	very, river
Zayin	ז	זאב	[z]	zebra, please
Zayin+geresh	ז׳	ז׳ורנל	[ʒ]	forge, pleasure
Chet	ח	חוט	[x]	as in Scots 'loch'
Tet	ט	טוב	[t]	tourist, trip
Yud	י	יום	[j]	yes, New York
Kaph	ך כ	כריש	[k]	clock, kiss
Lamed	ל	לחם	[l]	lace, people
Mem	ם מ	מלך	[m]	magic, milk
Nun	ן נ	נר	[n]	name, normal
Samech	ס	סוס	[s]	city, boss
Ayin	ע	עין	[ɑ], [ɑː]	bath, to pass
	ע	תָשְעִים	['] (ayn)	voiced pharyngeal fricative
Pei	ף פ	פיל	[p]	pencil, private
Tsadi	צ ץ	צעצוע	[ts]	cats, tsetse fly
Tsadi+geresh	צ׳י׳	צְ׳ק	[tʃ]	church, French
Qoph	ק	קוף	[k]	clock, kiss
Resh	ר	רכבת	[r]	French (guttural) R
Shin	ש	שלחן, עָשׂרִים	[s], [ʃ]	city, machine
Tav	ת	תפוז	[t]	tourist, trip

LIST OF ABBREVIATIONS

Explication

⇨ man	-	addressing a man
⇨ woman	-	addressing a woman
couple, men ⇨	-	a couple or men are speaking
man ⇨	-	man is speaking
man ⇨ man	-	a man speaks to a man
man ⇨ woman	-	a man speaks to a woman
woman ⇨	-	woman is speaking
woman ⇨ man	-	a woman speaks to a man
woman ⇨ woman	-	a woman speaks to a woman
women ⇨	-	women are speaking

English abbreviations

ab.	-	about
adj	-	adjective
adv	-	adverb
anim.	-	animate
as adj	-	attributive noun used as adjective
e.g.	-	for example
etc.	-	et cetera
fam.	-	familiar
fem.	-	feminine
form.	-	formal
inanim.	-	inanimate
masc.	-	masculine
math	-	mathematics
mil.	-	military
n	-	noun
pl	-	plural
pron.	-	pronoun
sb	-	somebody
sing.	-	singular
sth	-	something
v aux	-	auxiliary verb

vi	-	intransitive verb
vi, vt	-	intransitive, transitive verb
vt	-	transitive verb

Hebrew abbreviations

ז	-	masculine
ז"ר	-	masculine plural
ז, נ	-	masculine, feminine
נ	-	feminine
נ"ר	-	feminine plural

T&P BOOKS

HEBREW PHRASEBOOK

This section contains
important phrases that may
come in handy in various
real-life situations.
The phrasebook will help
you ask for directions, clarify
a price, buy tickets, and
order food at a restaurant

T&P Books Publishing

PHRASEBOOK
CONTENTS

T&P Books Publishing

The bare minimum

Excuse me, ... (⇨ man)	slaχ li, ... **‏סלח לי, ...‏**
Excuse me, ... (⇨ woman)	silχi li, ... **‏סלחי לי, ...‏**
Hello.	ʃalom. **‏שלום.‏**
Thank you.	toda. **‏תודה.‏**
Good bye.	lehitra'ot. **‏להתראות.‏**
Yes.	ken. **‏כן.‏**
No.	lo. **‏לא.‏**
I don't know. (man ⇨)	ani lo yo'deʿa. **‏אני לא יודע.‏**
I don't know. (woman ⇨)	ani lo yo'daʿat. **‏אני לא יודעת.‏**
Where? | Where to? | When?	eifo? | le'an? | matai? **?‏איפה? | לאן? | מתי?**
I need ... (man ⇨)	ani tsariχ ... **‏אני צריך ...‏**
I need ... (woman ⇨)	ani tsriχa ... **‏אני צריכה ...‏**
I want ... (man ⇨)	ani rotse ... **‏אני רוצה ...‏**
I want ... (woman ⇨)	ani rotsa ... **‏אני רוצה ...‏**
Do you have ...? (⇨ man)	ha'im yeʃ leχa ...? **?‏האם יש לך ...?**
Do you have ...? (⇨ woman)	ha'im yeʃ laχ ...? **?‏האם יש לך ...?**
Is there a ... here?	ha'im yeʃ po ...? **?‏האם יש פה ...?**
May I ...? (man ⇨)	ha'im ani yaχol ...? **?‏האם אני יכול ...?**
May I ...? (woman ⇨)	ha'im ani yeχola ...? **?‏האם אני יכולה ...?**
..., please (polite request)	..., bevakaʃa **‏..., בבקשה‏**

I'm looking for ... (man ⇨)	ani meχapes ... **אני מחפש ...**
I'm looking for ... (woman ⇨)	ani meχa'peset ... **אני מחפשת ...**
the restroom	ʃerutim **שירותים**
an ATM	kaspomat **כספומט**
a pharmacy (drugstore)	beit mer'kaχat **בית מרקחת**
a hospital	beit χolim **בית חולים**
the police station	taχanat miʃtara **תחנת משטרה**
the subway	ra'kevet taχtit **רכבת תחתית**
a taxi	monit, 'teksi **מונית, טקסי**
the train station	taχanat ra'kevet **תחנת רכבת**

My name is ...	kor'im li ... **קוראים לי ...**
What's your name? (⇨ man)	eiχ kor'im leχa? **איך קוראים לך?**
What's your name? (⇨ woman)	eiχ kor'im laχ? **איך קוראים לך?**
Could you please help me? (⇨ man)	ha'im ata yaχol la'azor li? **האם אתה יכול לעזור לי?**
Could you please help me? (⇨ woman)	ha'im at yeχola la'azor li? **האם את יבולה לעזור לי?**
I've got a problem.	yeʃ li be'aya. **יש לי בעייה.**
I don't feel well. (man ⇨)	ani lo margiʃ tov. **אני לא מרגיש טוב.**
I don't feel well. (woman ⇨)	ani lo margiʃa tov. **אני לא מרגישה טוב.**
Call an ambulance! (⇨ man)	hazmen 'ambulans! **הזמן אמבולנס!**
Call an ambulance! (⇨ woman)	haz'mini 'ambulans! **הזמיני אמבולנס!**
May I make a call? (man ⇨)	ha'im ani yaχol lehitkaʃer? **האם אני יכול להתקשר?**
May I make a call? (woman ⇨)	ha'im ani yeχola lehitkaʃer? **האם אני יכולה להתקשר?**

I'm sorry. (man ⇨)	ani mitsta'er. **אני מצטער.**
I'm sorry. (woman ⇨)	ani mitsta''eret. **אני מצטערת.**
You're welcome.	ein be'ad ma, bevakaʃa. **אין בעד מה, בבקשה.**

I, me	ani אני
you (inform.) (masc.)	ata אתה
you (inform.) (fem.)	at את
he	hu הוא
she	hi היא
they (masc.)	hem הם
they (fem.)	hen הן
we	a'naχnu אנחנו
you (pl) (masc.)	atem אתם
you (pl) (fem.)	aten אתן
you (sg, form.) (masc.)	ata אתה
you (sg, form.) (fem.)	at את

ENTRANCE	knisa כניסה
EXIT	yetsi'a יציאה
OUT OF ORDER	lo po'el לא פועל
CLOSED	sagur סגור
OPEN	pa'tuaχ פתוח
FOR WOMEN	lenaʃim לנשים
FOR MEN	ligvarim לגברים

Questions

Where?	eifo? **איפה?**
Where to?	le'an? **לאן?**
Where from?	me''eifo? **מאיפה?**
Why?	lama? **למה?**
For what reason?	me'eizo siba? **מאיזו סיבה?**
When?	matai? **מתי?**

How long?	kama zman? **כמה זמן?**
At what time?	be''eizo ʃa'a? **באיזו שעה?**
How much?	kama? **כמה?**
Do you have …? (⇨ man)	ha'im yeʃ leχa …? **האם יש לך ...?**
Do you have …? (⇨ woman)	ha'im yeʃ laχ …? **האם יש לך ...?**
Where is …?	eifo …? **איפה ...?**

What time is it?	ma haʃa'a? **מה השעה?**
May I make a call? (man ⇨)	ha'im ani yaχol lehitkaʃer? **האם אני יבול להתקשר?**
May I make a call? (woman ⇨)	ha'im ani yeχola lehitkaʃer? **האם אני יבולה להתקשר?**
Who's there?	mi ʃam? **מי שם?**
Can I smoke here?	ha'im mutar le'aʃen kan? **האם מותר לעשן כאן?**
May I …? (man ⇨)	ha'im ani yaχol …? **האם אני יבול ...?**
May I …? (woman ⇨)	ha'im ani yeχola …? **האם אני יבולה ...?**

Needs

I'd like … (man ⇨)	ha'yiti rotse … היתי רוצה …
I'd like … (woman ⇨)	ha'yiti rotsa … היתי רוצה …
I don't want … (man ⇨)	ani lo rotse … אני לא רוצה …
I don't want … (woman ⇨)	ani lo rotsa … אני לא רוצה …
I'm thirsty. (man ⇨)	ani tsame. אני צמא.
I'm thirsty. (woman ⇨)	ani tsme'a. אני צמאה.
I want to sleep.	ani rotse liſon. אני רוצה לישון.
I want … (man ⇨)	ani rotse … אני רוצה …
I want … (woman ⇨)	ani rotsa … אני רוצה …

to wash up	liſtof panim veya'dayim לשטוף פנים וידיים
to brush my teeth	letsax'tseax ʃi'nayim לצחצח שיניים
to rest a while	la'nuax ktsat לנוח קצת
to change my clothes	lehaxlif bgadim להחליף בגדים
to go back to the hotel	laxazor lamalon לחזור למלון
to buy …	liknot … לקנות …
to go to …	la'lexet le… ללכת ל …
to visit …	levaker be… לבקר ב …
to meet with …	lehipageʃ im… להיפגש עם…
to make a call	letalfen, lehitkaʃer לטלפן, להתקשר

I'm tired. (man ⇨)	ani ayef. אני עייף.
I'm tired. (woman ⇨)	ani ayefa. אני עייפה.

We are tired. (couple , men ⇨)	a'naχnu ayefim. **אנחנו עייפים.**
We are tired. (women ⇨)	anaχnu ayefot. **אנחנו עייפות.**
I'm cold.	kar li. **קר לי.**
I'm hot.	χam li. **חם לי.**
I'm OK.	ani be'seder. **אני בסדר.**

I need to make a call. (man ⇨)	ani tsariχ lehitkaʃer. **אני צריך להתקשר.**
I need to make a call. (woman ⇨)	ani tsriχa lehitkaʃer. **אני צריכה להתקשר.**
I need to go to the restroom. (man ⇨)	ani tsariχ leʃerutim. **אני צריך ללכת לשירותים.**
I need to go to the restroom. (woman ⇨)	ani tsriχa leʃerutim. **אני צריכה ללכת לשירותים.**
I have to go. (man ⇨)	ani tsariχ la'leχet. **אני צריך ללכת.**
I have to go. (woman ⇨)	ani tsriχa la'leχet. **אני צריכה ללכת.**
I have to go now. (man ⇨)	ani χayav la'leχet aχʃav. **אני חייב ללכת עכשיו.**
I have to go now. (woman ⇨)	ani χa'yevet la'leχet aχʃav. **אני חייבת ללכת עכשיו.**

Asking for directions

Excuse me, ... (man ⇨)	slaχ li, ... **... ,סלח לי**
Excuse me, ... (woman ⇨)	silχi li, ... **... ,סלחי לי**
Where is ...?	eifo ...? **?... איפה**
Which way is ...?	eiχ megi'im le ...? **?... איך מגיעים ל**
Could you help me, please? (⇨ man)	ha'im ata yaχol la'azor li, bevakaʃa? **?האם אתה יכול לעזור לי, בבקשה**
Could you help me, please? (⇨ woman)	ha'im at yeχola la'azor li, bevakaʃa? **?האם את יכולה לעזור לי, בבקשה**

I'm looking for ... (man ⇨)	ani meχapes ... **... אני מחפש**
I'm looking for ... (woman ⇨)	ani meχa'peset ... **... אני מחפשת**
I'm looking for the exit. (man ⇨)	ani meχapes et hayetsi'a. **.אני מחפש את היציאה**
I'm looking for the exit. (woman ⇨)	ani meχa'peset et hayetsi'a. **.אני מחפשת את היציאה**
I'm going to ... (man ⇨)	ani holeχ le ... **... אני הולך ל**
I'm going to ... (woman ⇨)	ani ho'leχet le ... **... אני הולכת ל**
Am I going the right way to ...?	ha'im ani bakivun hanaχon le ...? **?... האם אני בביוון הנכון ל**

Is it far?	ha'im ze raχok? **?האם זה רחוק**
Can I get there on foot?	ha'im efʃar leha'gi'a leʃam ba'regel? **?האם אפשר להגיע לשם ברגל**
Can you show me on the map? (⇨ man)	ha'im ata yaχol lehar'ot li al hamapa? **?האם אתה יכול להראות לי על המפה**
Can you show me on the map? (⇨ woman)	ha'im at yeχola lehar'ot li al hamapa? **?האם את יכולה להראות לי על המפה**
Show me where we are right now. (⇨ man)	har'e li heiχan 'anu nimtsa'im aχʃav. **.הראה לי היכן אנו נמצאים עכשיו**
Show me where we are right now. (⇨ woman)	har'i li heiχan 'anu nimtsa'im aχʃav. **.הראי לי היכן אנו נמצאים עכשיו**
Here	kan, po **כאן, פה**
There	ʃam **שם**

This way	lekan
	לכאן
Turn right. (⇨ man)	pne ya'mina.
	פנה ימינה.
Turn right. (⇨ woman)	pni ya'mina.
	פני ימינה.
Turn left. (⇨ man)	pne 'smola.
	פנה שמאלה.
Turn left. (⇨ woman)	pni 'smola.
	פני שמאלה.
first (second, third) turn	pniya riʃona (ʃniya, ʃliʃit)
	פנייה ראשונה (שנייה, שלישית)
to the right	ya'mina
	ימינה
to the left	smola
	שמאלה
Go straight ahead. (⇨ man)	leχ yaʃar.
	לך ישר.
Go straight ahead. (⇨ woman)	leχi yaʃar.
	לכי ישר.

Signs

WELCOME!	bruχim haba'im! ברוכים הבאים!
ENTRANCE	knisa כניסה
EXIT	yetsi'a יציאה
PUSH	dχof דחוף
PULL	mʃoχ משוך
OPEN	pa'tuaχ פתוח
CLOSED	sagur סגור
FOR WOMEN	lenaʃim לנשים
FOR MEN	ligvarim לגברים
GENTLEMEN, GENTS	gvarim גברים
WOMEN	naʃim נשים
DISCOUNTS	hanaχot הנחות
SALE	mivtsa מבצע
FREE	χinam, beχinam חינם, בחינם
NEW!	χadaʃ! חדש!
ATTENTION!	sim lev! שים לב!
NO VACANCIES	ein mekomot pnuyim אין מקומות פנויים
RESERVED	ʃamur שמור
ADMINISTRATION	hanhala הנהלה
STAFF ONLY	le'ovdim bilvad לעובדים בלבד

BEWARE OF THE DOG!	zehirut, 'kelev! זהירות כלב!
NO SMOKING!	asur le'aʃen! אסור לעשן!
DO NOT TOUCH!	asur la'ga'at! אסור לגעת!
DANGEROUS	mesukan מסוכן
DANGER	sakana סכנה
HIGH VOLTAGE	metaχ ga'voha מתח גבוה
NO SWIMMING!	asur lisχot! אסור לשחות!
OUT OF ORDER	lo po'el לא פועל
FLAMMABLE	dalik דליק
FORBIDDEN	asur אסור
NO TRESPASSING!	ein ma'avar אין מעבר
WET PAINT	tseva laχ, 'tseva tari צבע לח, צבע טרי
CLOSED FOR RENOVATIONS	sagur leʃiputsim סגור לשיפוצים
WORKS AHEAD	avodot bakviʃ עבודות בכביש
DETOUR	ma'akaf מעקף

Transportation. General phrases

plane	matos
	מטוס
train	ra'kevet
	רכבת
bus	'otobus
	אוטובוס
ferry	ma'a'boret
	מעבורת
taxi	monit
	מונית
car	meχonit
	מכונית

schedule	luaχ zmanim
	לוח זמנים
Where can I see the schedule?	heiχan efʃar lir'ot et 'luaχ hazmanim?
	היכן אפשר לראות את לוח הזמנים?
workdays (weekdays)	yemei avoda
	ימי עבודה
weekends	sofei ʃa'vu'a
	סופי שבוע
holidays	χagim
	חגים

DEPARTURE	hamra'a
	המראה
ARRIVAL	neχita
	נחיתה
DELAYED	ikuv
	עיכוב
CANCELLED	bitul
	ביטול

next (train, etc.)	haba /haba'a/
	הבא /הבאה/
first	riʃon /riʃona/
	ראשון /ראשונה/
last	aχaron /aχrona/
	אחרון /אחרונה/

When is the next ...?	matai ha... haba /haba'a/?
	מתי ה ... הבא /הבאה/?
When is the first ...?	matai ha... hariʃon /hariʃona/?
	מתי ה ... הראשון /הראשונה/?

When is the last ...?	matai ha... ha'aχaron /ha'aχrona/?
	מתי ה ... האחרון /האחרונה/?
transfer (change of trains, etc.)	haχlafa, ko'nekʃen
	החלפה, קונקשן
to make a transfer	la'asot haχlafa
	לעשות החלפה
Do I need to make a transfer? (man ⇨)	ha'im ani tsariχ la'asot haχlafa?
	האם אני צריך לעשות החלפה?
Do I need to make a transfer? (woman ⇨)	ha'im ani tsriχa la'asot haχlafa?
	האם אני צריכה לעשות החלפה?

Buying tickets

Where can I buy tickets?	heixan effar liknot kartisim? היכן אפשר לקנות כרטיסים?
ticket	kartis כרטיס
to buy a ticket	liknot kartis לקנות כרטיס
ticket price	mexir kartis מחיר כרטיס

Where to?	le'an? לאן?
To what station?	le"eizo taxana? לאיזו תחנה?
I need ... (man ⇨)	ani tsarix ... אני צריך ...
I need ... (woman ⇨)	ani tsrixa ... אני צריבה ...
one ticket	kartis exad כרטיס אחד
two tickets	ʃnei kartisim שני כרטיסים
three tickets	ʃloʃa kartisim שלושה כרטיסים

one-way	kivun exad כיוון אחד
round-trip	halox vaʃov הלוך ושוב
first class	maxlaka riʃona מחלקה ראשונה
second class	maxlaka ʃniya מחלקה שנייה
today	hayom היום
tomorrow	maxar מחר
the day after tomorrow	maxara'tayim מחרתיים
in the morning	ba'boker בבוקר
in the afternoon	axar hatsaha'rayim אחר הצהריים
in the evening	ba"erev בערב

aisle seat	moʃav bamaʿavar
	מושב במעבר
window seat	moʃav leyad haχalon
	מושב ליד החלון
How much?	kama?
	?כמה
Can I pay by credit card?	ha'im efʃar leʃalem bekatrtis aʃrai?
	?האם אפשר לשלם בברטיס אשראי

Bus

bus	'otobus אוטובוס
intercity bus	'otobus bein ironi אוטובוס בין-עירוני
bus stop	taxanat 'otobus תחנת אוטובוס
Where's the nearest bus stop?	eifo taxanat ha''otobus hakrova beyoter? איפה תחנת האוטובוס הקרובה ביותר?
number (bus ~, etc.)	mispar מספר
Which bus do I take to get to …?	eize 'otobus tsarix la'kaxat kedei leha'gi'a le …? איזה אוטובוס צריך לקחת כדי להגיע ל …?
Does this bus go to …?	ha'im ha''otobus haze ma'gi'a le …? האם האוטובוס הזה מגיע ל …?
How frequent are the buses?	ma hatadirut ʃel ha'oto'busim? מה התדירות של האוטובוסים?
every 15 minutes	kol xameʃ esre dakot כל חמש עשרה דקות
every half hour	kol xatsi ʃa'a כל חצי שעה
every hour	kol ʃa'a כל שעה
several times a day	mispar pe'amim beyom מספר פעמים ביום
… times a day	… pe'amim beyom … פעמים ביום
schedule	luax zmanim לוח זמנים
Where can I see the schedule?	heixan efʃar lir'ot et 'luax hazmanim? היכן אפשר לראות את לוח הזמנים?
When is the next bus?	matai ha''otobus haba? מתי האוטובוס הבא?
When is the first bus?	matai ha''otobus hariʃon? מתי האוטובוס הראשון?
When is the last bus?	matai ha''otobus ha'axaron? מתי האוטובוס האחרון?

stop	taχanat atsira **תחנת עצירה**
next stop	hataχana haba'a **התחנה הבאה**
last stop (terminus)	taχana aχrona **תחנה אחרונה**
Stop here, please. (⇨ man)	atsor kan, bevakaʃa. **עצור כאן, בבקשה.**
Stop here, please. (⇨ woman)	itsri kan, bevakaʃa. **עצרי כאן, בבקשה.**
Excuse me, this is my stop. (⇨ man)	slaχ li, zo hataχana ʃeli. **סלח לי, זו התחנה שלי.**
Excuse me, this is my stop. (⇨ woman)	silχi li, zo hataχana ʃeli. **סלחי לי, זו התחנה שלי.**

Train

train	ra'kevet
	רכבת
suburban train	ra'kevet parvarim
	רכבת פרברים
long-distance train	ra'kevet bein ironit
	רכבת בין-עירונית
train station	taxanat ra'kevet
	תחנת רכבת
Excuse me, where is the exit to the platform? (⇨ man)	slax li, 'eifo hayetsi'a laratsif?
	סלח לי, איפה היציאה לרציף?
Excuse me, where is the exit to the platform? (⇨ woman)	silxi li, 'eifo hayetsi'a laratsif?
	סלחי לי, איפה היציאה לרציף?
Does this train go to …?	ha'im hara'kevet hazo megi'a le …?
	האם הרכבת הזו מגיעה ל …?
next train	hara'kevet haba'a
	הרכבת הבאה
When is the next train?	matai hara'kevet haba'a?
	מתי הרכבת הבאה?
Where can I see the schedule?	heixan efʃar lir'ot et 'luax hazmanim?
	היכן אפשר לראות את לוח הזמנים?
From which platform?	me''eize ratsif?
	מאיזה רציף?
When does the train arrive in …?	matai hara'kevet megi'a le …?
	מתי הרכבת מגיעה ל …?
Please help me. (⇨ man)	azor li bevakaʃa.
	עזור לי בבקשה.
Please help me. (⇨ woman)	izri li bevakaʃa.
	עזרי לי בבקשה.
I'm looking for my seat. (man ⇨)	ani mexapes et hamoʃav ʃeli.
	אני מחפש את המושב שלי.
I'm looking for my seat. (woman ⇨)	ani mexa'peset et hamoʃav ʃeli.
	אני מחפשת את המושב שלי.
We're looking for our seats. (couple , men ⇨)	anu mexapsim et hamoʃavim ʃe'lanu
	אנו מחפשים את המושבים שלנו.
We're looking for our seats. (women ⇨)	anu mexapsot et hamoʃavim ʃe'lanu
	אנו מחפשות את המושבים שלנו.
My seat is taken.	hamoʃav ʃeli tafus.
	המושב שלי תפוס.
Our seats are taken.	hamoʃavim ʃe'lanu tfusim.
	המושבים שלנו תפוסים.
I'm sorry but this is my seat. (man ⇨)	ani mitsta'er, aval ze hamoʃav ʃeli.
	אני מצטער, אבל זה המושב שלי.

I'm sorry but this is my seat. (woman ⇨)

ani mitsta"eret, aval ze hamoʃav ʃeli.
אני מצטערת, אבל זה המושב שלי.

Is this seat taken?

ha'im hamoʃav haze tafus?
האם המושב הזה תפוס?

May I sit here? (man ⇨)

ha'im ani yaχol la'ʃevet kan?
האם אני יכול לשבת כאן?

May I sit here? (woman ⇨)

ha'im ani yeχola laʃevet kan?
האם אני יכולה לשבת כאן?

On the train. Dialogue (No ticket)

Ticket, please.	kartis, bevakaʃa. כרטיס, בבקשה.
I don't have a ticket.	ein li kartis. אין לי כרטיס.
I lost my ticket.	i'badti et hakartis ʃeli. איבדתי את הכרטיס שלי.
I forgot my ticket at home.	ʃa'xaxti et hakartis ʃeli ba'bayit שכחתי את הכרטיס שלי בבית.

You can buy a ticket from me. (⇨ man)	ata yaxol liknot kartis mi'meni. אתה יכול לקנות כרטיס ממני.
You can buy a ticket from me. (⇨ woman)	at yexola liknot kartis mi'meni. את יכולה לקנות כרטיס ממני.
You will also have to pay a fine. (⇨ man)	titstarex gam leʃalem knas. תצטרך גם לשלם קנס.
You will also have to pay a fine. (⇨ woman)	titstarxi gam leʃalem knas. תצטרכי גם לשלם קנס.
Okay.	okei. אוקיי.
Where are you going? (⇨ man)	le'an ata no'seʿa? לאן אתה נוסע?
Where are you going? (⇨ woman)	le'an at nos'aʿat? לאן את נוסעת?
I'm going to ... (man ⇨)	ani no'seʿa le... אני נוסע ל...
I'm going to ... (woman ⇨)	ani nos'aʿat le... אני נוסעת ל...

How much? I don't understand. (man ⇨)	kama? ani lo mevin. כמה? אני לא מבין.
How much? I don't understand. (woman ⇨)	kama? ani lo mevina. כמה? אני לא מבינה.
Write it down, please. (⇨ man)	ktov li et ze, bevakaʃa. כתוב לי את זה, בבקשה.
Write it down, please. (⇨ woman)	kitvi li et ze, bevakaʃa. כתבי לי את זה, בבקשה.
Okay. Can I pay with a credit card?	okei. ha'im efʃar leʃalem bekartis aʃrai? אוקיי. האם אפשר לשלם בכרטיס אשראי?
Yes, you can.	ken, efʃar. כן, אפשר.
Here's your receipt. (⇨ man)	hine hakabala ʃelxa. הנה הקבלה שלך.
Here's your receipt. (⇨ woman)	hine hakabala ʃelax' הינה הקבלה שלך

Sorry about the fine. (man ⇨)

ani mitsta'er be'kefer laknas.
אני מצטער בקשר לקנס.

Sorry about the fine. (woman ⇨)

ani mitsta''eret be'kefer laknas.
אני מצטערת בקשר לקנס.

That's okay. It was my fault.

ze be'seder. zo afmati.
זה בסדר. זו אשמתי.

Enjoy your trip.

tiyul mehane.
טיול מהנה.

Taxi

taxi	monit
	מונית
taxi driver (masc.)	nahag monit
	נהג מונית
taxi driver (fem.)	na'heget monit
	נהגת מונית
to catch a taxi	litpos monit
	לתפוס מונית
taxi stand	taχanat moniyot
	תחנת מוניות
Where can I get a taxi?	eifo efʃar la'kaχat monit?
	איפה אפשר לקחת מונית?

to call a taxi	lehazmin monit
	להזמין מונית
I need a taxi. (man ⇨)	ani tsariχ monit
	אני צריך מונית
I need a taxi. (woman ⇨)	ani tsriχa monit
	אני צריכה מונית
Right now.	aχʃav.
	עכשיו.
What is your address (location)? (⇨ man)	ma ha'ktovet ʃelχa?
	מה הכתובת שלך?
What is your address (location)? (⇨ woman)	ma ha'ktovet ʃelaχ?
	מה הכתובת שלך?
My address is ...	ha'ktovet ʃeli hi ...
	הכתובת שלי היא ...
Your destination? (⇨ man)	le'an ata no'se'a?
	לאן אתה נוסע?
Your destination? (⇨ woman)	le'an at nos'a'at?
	לאן את נוסעת?

Excuse me, ... (⇨ man)	slaχ li, ...
	סלח לי, ...
Excuse me, ... (⇨ woman)	silχi li, ...
	סלחי לי, ...
Are you available? (⇨ man)	ha'im ata panui?
	האם אתה פנוי?
Are you available? (⇨ woman)	ha'im at pnuya?
	האם את פנויה?
How much is it to get to ...?	kama ze ole lin'so'a le ...?
	כמה זה עולה לנסוע ל ...?
Do you know where it is? (⇨ man)	ha'im ata yo'de'a 'eifo ze?
	האם אתה יודע איפה זה?

Do you know where it is? (⇨ woman)
ha'im at yod'a'at 'eifo ze?
האם את יודעת איפה זה?

Airport, please.
lisde hate'ufa, bevakaʃa.
לשדה התעופה, בבקשה.

Stop here, please. (⇨ man)
atsor kan, bevakaʃa.
עצור כאן, בבקשה.

Stop here, please. (⇨ woman)
itsri kan, bevakaʃa.
עצרי כאן, בבקשה.

It's not here.
ze lo kan.
זה לא כאן.

This is the wrong address.
zo lo ha'ktovet haneχona.
זו לא הכתובת הנכונה.

Turn left. (⇨ man)
pne 'smola.
פנה שמאלה.

Turn left. (⇨ woman)
pni 'smola.
פני שמאלה.

Turn right. (⇨ man)
pne ya'mina.
פנה ימינה.

Turn right. (⇨ woman)
pni ya'mina.
פני ימינה.

How much do I owe you? (man ⇨)
kama me'gi'a leχa?
כמה מגיע לך?

How much do I owe you? (woman ⇨)
kama me'gi'a laχ?
כמה מגיע לך?

I'd like a receipt, please.
efʃar lekabel kabala, bevakaʃa?
אפשר לקבל קבלה, בבקשה?

Keep the change. (⇨ man)
ʃmor et ha''odef.
שמור את העודף.

Keep the change. (⇨ woman)
ʃimri et ha''odef.
שמרי את העודף.

Would you please wait for me? (⇨ man)
ha'im ata muχan leχakot li, bevakaʃa?
האם אתה מוכן לחכות לי, בבקשה?

Would you please wait for me? (⇨ woman)
ha'im at muχana leχakot li, bevakaʃa?
האם את מוכנה לחכות לי, בבקשה?

five minutes
χameʃ dakot
חמש דקות

ten minutes
eser dakot
עשר דקות

fifteen minutes
χameʃ esre dakot
חמש עשרה דקות

twenty minutes
esrim dakot
עשרים דקות

half an hour
χatsi ʃa'a
חצי שעה

Hotel

Hello.	ʃalom. **שלום.**
My name is …	kor'im li … **קוראים לי ...**
I have a reservation.	yeʃ li hazmana. **יש לי הזמנה.**
I need … (man ⇨)	ani tsariҳ … **אני צריך ...**
I need … (woman ⇨)	ani tsriҳa … **אני צריכה ...**
a single room	ҳeder leyaҳid **חדר ליחיד**
a double room	ҳeder zugi **חדר זוגי**
How much is that?	kama ze ole? **כמה זה עולה?**
That's a bit expensive.	ze ktsat yakar. **זה קצת יקר.**
Do you have anything else? (⇨ man)	ha'im yeʃ leҳa 'optsiyot aҳerot? **האם יש לך אופציות אחרות?**
Do you have anything else? (⇨ woman)	ha'im yeʃ laҳ 'optsiyot aҳerot? **האם יש לך אופציות אחרות?**
I'll take it.	ani ekaҳ et ze. **אני אקח את זה.**
I'll pay in cash.	ani eʃalem bimzuman. **אני אשלם במזומן.**
I've got a problem.	yeʃ li be'aya. **יש לי בעיה.**
My … is broken. (masc.)	ha… ʃeli mekulkal. **ה... שלי מקולקל.**
My … is broken. (fem.)	ha… ʃeli mekul'kelet. **ה... שלי מקולקלת.**
My … is out of order. (masc.)	ha… ʃeli lo oved. **ה... שלי לא עובד.**
My … is out of order. (fem.)	ha… ʃeli lo o'vedet. **ה... שלי לא עובדת.**
TV	tele'vizya **טלוויזיה**
air conditioner	mizug avir **מיזוג אוויר**

tap	berez ברז
shower	mik'laχat מקלחת
sink	kiyor כיור
safe	ka'sefet כספת
door lock	man'ul מנעול
electrical outlet	ʃeka שקע
hairdryer	meyabeʃ se'ar מייבש שיער

I don't have …	ein li … אין לי ...
water	mayim מים
light	te'ura תאורה
electricity	χaʃmal חשמל

Can you give me …?	ha'im at yeχola latet li …? האם את יכולה לתת לי ...?
a towel	ma'gevet מגבת
a blanket	smiχa שמיכה
slippers	na'alei 'bayit נעלי בית
a robe	χaluk חלוק
shampoo	ʃampo שמפו
soap	sabon סבון

I'd like to change rooms. (man ⇨)	ani rotse lehaχlif 'χeder. אני רוצה להחליף חדר.
I'd like to change rooms. (woman ⇨)	ani rotsa lehaχlif 'χeder. אני רוצה להחליף חדר.
I can't find my key. (man ⇨)	ani lo motse et hamaf'teaχ ʃeli. אני לא מוצא את המפתח שלי.
I can't find my key. (woman ⇨)	ani lo motset et hamaf'teaχ ʃeli. אני לא מוצאת את המפתח שלי.
Could you open my room, please?	ha'im ata yaχol lif'toaχ et χadri, bevakaʃa? האם אתה יכול לפתוח את חדרי, בבקשה?

Who's there?	mi ʃam? **?מי שם**
Come in!	hikanes! **!היכנס**
Just a minute!	rak 'rega! **!רק רגע**
Not right now, please.	lo axʃav, bevakaʃa. **.לא עכשיו, בבקשה**

Come to my room, please.	bo'i lexadri, bevakaʃa. **.בואי לחדרי, בבקשה**
I'd like to order food service. (man ⇨)	ani mevakeʃ lehazmin ʃerut xadarim. **.אני מבקש להזמין שירות חדרים**
I'd like to order food service. (woman ⇨)	ani meva'keʃet lehazmin ʃerut xadarim. **.אני מבקשת להזמין שירות חדרים**
My room number is …	mispar ha'xeder ʃeli hu … **... מספר החדר שלי הוא**

I'm leaving … (man ⇨)	ani ozev … **... אני עוזב**
I'm leaving … (woman ⇨)	ani o'zevet … **... אני עוזבת**
We're leaving … (couple , men ⇨)	a'naxnu ozvim … **... אנחנו עוזבים**
We're leaving … (women ⇨)	a'naxnu ozvot … **... אנחנו עוזבות**

right now	axʃav **עכשיו**
this afternoon	axar hatsaha'rayim **אחר הצהריים**
tonight	ha'laila **הלילה**
tomorrow	maxar **מחר**
tomorrow morning	maxar ba'boker **מחר בבוקר**
tomorrow evening	maxar ba''erev **מחר בערב**
the day after tomorrow	maxara'tayim **מחרתיים**

I'd like to pay. (man ⇨)	ani rotse leʃalem. **.אני רוצה לשלם**
I'd like to pay. (woman ⇨)	ani rotsa leʃalem. **.אני רוצה לשלם**
Everything was wonderful.	hakol haya nehedar. **.הכל היה נהדר**
Where can I get a taxi?	eifo efʃar la'kaxat monit? **?איפה אפשר לקחת מונית**

Would you call a taxi for me, please?
(⇨ man)

ha'im ata yaχol lehazmin li monit, bevakaʃa?

האם אתה יכול להזמין לי מונית, בבקשה?

Would you call a taxi for me, please?
(⇨ woman)

ha'im at yeχola lehazmin li monit, bevakaʃa?

האם את יכולה להזמין לי מונית, בבקשה?

Restaurant

Can I look at the menu, please?	ha'im efʃar lekabel tafrit, bevakaʃa? **האם אפשר לקבל תפריט, בבקשה?**
Table for one.	ʃulχan leyaχid. **שולחן ליחיד.**
There are two (three, four) of us.	a'naχnu 'ʃnayim (ʃloʃa, arba'a). **אנחנו שניים (שלושה, ארבעה).**

Smoking	me'aʃnim **מעשנים**
No smoking	lo me'aʃnim **לא מעשנים**
Excuse me! (addressing a waiter) (⇨ man)	slaχ li! **סלח לי!**
Excuse me! (addressing a waiter) (⇨ woman)	silχi li! **סלחי לי!**
menu	tafrit **תפריט**
wine list	reʃimat yeinot **רשימת יינות**
The menu, please.	tafrit, bevakaʃa. **תפריט, בבקשה.**

Are you ready to order? (⇨ man)	ha'im ata muχan lehazmin? **האם אתה מוכן להזמין?**
Are you ready to order? (⇨ woman)	ha'im at muχana lehazmin? **האם את מוכנה להזמין?**
What will you have? (⇨ man)	ma tirtse? **מה תרצה?**
What will you have? (⇨ woman)	ma tirtsi? **מה תרצי?**
I'll have ... (man ⇨)	ani rotse ... **אני רוצה ...**
I'll have ... (woman ⇨)	ani rotsa ... **אני רוצה ...**
I'm a vegetarian. (man ⇨)	ani tsimχoni. **אני צמחוני.**
I'm a vegetarian. (woman ⇨)	ani tsimχonit. **אני צמחונית.**
meat	basar **בשר**
fish	dagim **דגים**
vegetables	yerakot **ירקות**

Do you have vegetarian dishes?

ha'im yeʃ laχem manot tsimχoniyot?
האם יש לכם מנות צמחוניות?

I don't eat pork. (man ⇨)

ani lo oχel χazir.
אני לא אוכל חזיר.

I don't eat pork. (woman ⇨)

ani lo o'χelet χazir.
אני לא אוכלת חזיר.

He doesn't eat meat.

hu lo oχel basar.
הוא לא אוכל בשר.

She doesn't eat meat.

hi lo o'χelet basar.
היא לא אוכלת בשר.

I am allergic to … (man ⇨)

ani a'lergi le…
אני אלרגי ל...

I am allergic to … (woman ⇨)

ani a'lergit le…
אני אלרגית ל...

Would you please bring me … (⇨ man)

ha'im ata yaχol lehavi li, bevakaʃa, …
האם אתה יכול להביא לי, בבקשה, ...

Would you please bring me … (⇨ woman)

ha'im at yeχola lehavi li, bevakaʃa, …
האם את יבולה להביא לי, בבקשה, ...

salt | pepper | sugar

melaχ | 'pilpel | sukar
מלח | פלפל | סוכר

coffee | tea | dessert

kafe | te | ki'nuaχ
קפה | תה | קינוח

water | sparkling | plain

mayim | mugazim | regilim
מים | מוגזים| רגילים

a spoon | fork | knife

kaf | mazleg | sakin
כף | מזלג | סכין

a plate | napkin

tsa'laχat | mapit
צלחת | מפית

Enjoy your meal!

bete'avon!
בתיאבון!

One more, please.

od eχad /aχat/, bevakaʃa.
עוד אחד /אחת/, בבקשה.

It was very delicious.

ze haya me'od ta'im.
זה היה מאוד טעים.

---

check | change | tip

χeʃbon | 'odef | tip
חשבון | עודף | טיפ

Check, please.
(Could I have the check, please?)

χeʃbon, bevakaʃa.
חשבון, בבקשה.

Can I pay by credit card?

ha'im efʃar leʃalem bekatrtis aʃrai?
האם אפשר לשלם בכרטיס אשראי?

I'm sorry, there's a mistake here.
(man ⇨)

ani mitsta'er, yeʃ kan ta'ut.
אני מצטער, יש כאן טעות.

I'm sorry, there's a mistake here.
(woman ⇨)

ani mitsta''eret, yeʃ kan ta'ut.
אני מצטערת, יש כאן טעות.

Shopping

Can I help you? (⇨ man)	ha'im efʃar la'azor leχa? האם אפשר לעזור לך?
Can I help you? (⇨ woman)	ha'im efʃar la'azor laχ? האם אפשר לעזור לך?
Do you have ...?	ha'im yeʃ laχem ...? האם יש לכם ...?
I'm looking for ... (man ⇨)	ani meχapes ... אני מחפש ...
I'm looking for ... (woman ⇨)	ani meχa'peset ... אני מחפשת ...
I need ... (man ⇨)	ani tsariχ ... אני צריך ...
I need ... (woman ⇨)	ani tsriχa ... אני צריכה ...

I'm just looking. (man ⇨)	ani rak mistakel. אני רק מסתכל.
I'm just looking. (woman ⇨)	ani rak mista'kelet. אני רק מסתכלת.
We're just looking. (couple , men ⇨)	a'naχnu rak mistaklim. אנחנו רק מסתכלים.
We're just looking. (women ⇨)	a'naχnu rak mistaklot. אנחנו רק מסתכלות.
I'll come back later.	ani aχazor me'uχar yoter. אני אחזור מאוחר יותר.
We'll come back later.	a'naχnu naχazor me'uχar yoter. אנחנו נחזור מאוחר יותר.
discounts	sale	hanaχot	mivtsa הנחות	מבצע

Would you please show me ... (⇨ man)	ha'im ata yaχol lehar'ot li ... האם אתה יכול להראות לי ...
Would you please show me ... (⇨ woman)	ha'im at yeχola lehar'ot li ... האם את יכולה להראות לי ...
Would you please give me ... (⇨ man)	ha'im ata yaχol latet li, bevakaʃa ... האם אתה יכול לתת לי, בבקשה ...
Would you please give me ... (⇨ woman)	ha'im at yeχola latet li, bevakaʃa ... האם את יכולה לתת לי, בבקשה ...
Can I try it on? (man ⇨)	ha'im ani yaχol limdod et ze? האם אני יכול למדוד את זה?
Can I try it on? (woman ⇨)	ha'im ani yeχola limdod et ze? האם אני יכולה למדוד את זה?

Excuse me, where's the fitting room?
(⇨ man)
slaχ li, 'eifo χadar hahalbaʃa?
סלח לי, איפה חדר ההלבשה?

Excuse me, where's the fitting room?
(⇨ woman)
silχi li, 'eifo χadar hahalbaʃa?
סלחי לי, איפה חדר ההלבשה?

Which color would you like? (⇨ man)
eize 'tseva ha'yita rotse?
איזה צבע היית רוצה?

Which color would you like? (⇨ woman)
eize 'tseva hayit rotsa?
איזה צבע היית רוצה?

size | length
mida | 'oreχ
מידה | אורך

How does it fit? (⇨ man)
ha'im ze mat'im leχa?
האם זה מתאים לך?

How does it fit? (⇨ woman)
ha'im ze mat'im laχ?
האם זה מתאים לך?

How much is it?
kama ze ole?
במה זה עולה?

That's too expensive.
ze yakar midai.
זה יקר מידי.

I'll take it.
ani ekaχ et ze.
אני אקח את זה.

Excuse me, where do I pay? (man ⇨)
slaχ li, 'eifo meʃalmim?
סלח לי, איפה משלמים?

Excuse me, where do I pay? (woman ⇨)
silχi li, 'eifo 'meʃalmim?
סלחי לי, איפה משלמים?

Will you pay in cash or credit card?
(⇨ man)
ha'im ata meʃalem bimzuman
o bekartis aʃrai?
האם אתה משלם במזומן
או בכרטיס אשראי?

Will you pay in cash or credit card?
(⇨ woman)
ha'im at meʃa'lemet bimzuman
o bekartis aʃrai?
האם את משלמת במזומן
או בכרטיס אשראי?

In cash | with credit card
bimzuman | bekartis aʃrai
במזומן | בכרטיס אשראי

Do you want the receipt? (⇨ man)
ha'im ata rotse et hakabala?
האם אתה רוצה את הקבלה?

Do you want the receipt? (⇨ woman)
ha'im at rotsa et hakabala?
האם את רוצה את הקבלה?

Yes, please.
ken, bevakaʃa.
כן, בבקשה.

No, it's OK.
lo, ze be'seder.
לא, זה בסדר.

Thank you. Have a nice day! (⇨ man)
toda. ʃeyihye leχa yom na'im!
תודה. שיהיה לך יום נעים!

Thank you. Have a nice day! (⇨ woman)
toda. ʃeyihye laχ yom na'im!
תודה. שיהיה לך יום נעים!

In town

Excuse me, please. (⇨ man)	slaχ li, bevakaʃa.
	סלח לי, בבקשה.
Excuse me, please. (⇨ woman)	silχi li, bevakaʃa.
	סלחי לי, בבקשה.
I'm looking for ... (man ⇨)	ani meχapes ...
	אני מחפש ...
I'm looking for ... (woman ⇨)	ani meχa'peset ...
	אני מחפשת ...
the subway	ra'kevet taχtit
	רכבת תחתית
my hotel	et hamalon ʃeli
	את המלון שלי
the movie theater	et hakol'no'a
	את הקולנוע
a taxi stand	taχanat moniyot
	תחנת מוניות
an ATM	kaspomat
	כספומט
a foreign exchange office	misrad mat'be'a χuts
	משרד מטבע חוץ
an internet café	beit kafe 'internet
	בית קפה אינטרנט
... street	reχov ...
	רחוב ...
this place	hamakom haze
	המקום הזה
Do you know where ... is? (⇨ man)	ha'im ata yo'de'a heiχan nimtsa ...?
	האם אתה יודע היכן נמצא ...?
Do you know where ... is? (⇨ woman)	ha'im at yo'da'at heiχan nimtsa ...?
	האם את יודעת היכן נמצא ...?
Which street is this?	eize reχov ze?
	איזה רחוב זה?
Show me where we are right now. (⇨ man)	har'e li heiχan 'anu nimtsa'im aχʃav.
	הראה לי היכן אנו נמצאים עכשיו.
Show me where we are right now. (⇨ woman)	har'i li heiχan anu nimtsa'im aχʃav.
	הראי לי היכן אנו נמצאים עכשיו.
Can I get there on foot?	ha'im efʃar leha'gi'a leʃam ba'regel?
	האם אפשר להגיע לשם ברגל?
Do you have a map of the city? (⇨ man)	ha'im yeʃ leχa mapa ʃel ha'ir?
	האם יש לך מפה של העיר?
Do you have a map of the city? (⇨ woman)	ha'im yeʃ laχ mapa ʃel ha'ir?
	האם יש לך מפה של העיר?

How much is a ticket to get in?

kama ole kartis knisa?
כמה עולה כרטיס כניסה?

Can I take pictures here?

ha'im mutar letsalem kan?
האם מותר לצלם כאן?

Are you open?

ha'im atem ptuχim?
האם אתם פתוחים?

When do you open?

matai atem potχim?
מתי אתם פותחים?

When do you close?

matai atem sogrim?
מתי אתם סוגרים?

Money

money	kesef
	כסף
cash	mezuman
	מזומן
paper money	ʃtarot 'kesef
	שטרות כסף
loose change	kesef katan
	כסף קטן
check | change | tip	xeʃbon | 'odef | tip
	חשבון | עודף | טיפ

credit card	kartis aʃrai
	כרטיס אשראי
wallet	arnak
	ארנק
to buy	liknot
	לקנות
to pay	leʃalem
	לשלם
fine	knas
	קנס
free	xinam
	חינם

Where can I buy …?	eifo efʃar liknot …?
	איפה אפשר לקנות ...?
Is the bank open now?	ha'im ha'bank pa'tuax axʃav?
	האם הבנק פתוח עכשיו?
When does it open?	matai ze nisgar?
	מתי זה נפתח?
When does it close?	matai ze niftax?
	מתי זה נסגר?

How much?	kama?
	כמה?
How much is this?	kama ze ole?
	כמה זה עולה?
That's too expensive.	ze yakar midai.
	זה יקר מידי.

Excuse me, where do I pay?	slixa, 'eifo meʃalmim?
	סליחה, איפה משלמים?
Check, please.	xeʃbon, bevakaʃa.
	חשבון, בבקשה.

Can I pay by credit card?
ha'im efʃar leʃalem bekatrtis aʃrai?
האם אפשר לשלם בברטיס אשראי?

Is there an ATM here?
ha'im yeʃ kan kaspomat?
האם יש כאן בספומט?

I'm looking for an ATM. (man ⇨)
ani meχapes kaspomat.
אני מחפש בספומט.

I'm looking for an ATM. (woman ⇨)
ani meχa'peset kaspomat.
אני מחפשת בספומט.

I'm looking for a foreign exchange office. (man ⇨)
ani meχapes misrad mat'be'a χuts.
אני מחפש משרד מטבע חוץ.

I'm looking for a foreign exchange office. (woman ⇨)
ani meχa'peset misrad mat'be'a χuts.
אני מחפשת משרד מטבע חוץ.

I'd like to change ... (man ⇨)
ani rotse lehaχlif ...
אני רוצה להחליף ...

I'd like to change ... (woman ⇨)
ani rotsa lehaχlif ...
אני רוצה להחליף ...

What is the exchange rate?
ma 'ʃa'ar haχalifin?
מה שער החליפין?

Do you need my passport? (⇨ man)
ha'im ata tsariχ et hadarkon ʃeli?
האם אתה צריך את הדרכון שלי?

Do you need my passport? (⇨ woman)
ha'im at tsriχa et hadarkon ʃeli?
האם את צריכה את הדרכון שלי?

Time

What time is it?	ma haʃa'a? מה השעה?
When?	matai? מתי?
At what time?	be''eizo ʃa'a? באיזו שעה?
now | later | after …	axʃav | axar kax | axrei … עכשיו | אחר כך | אחרי ...
one o'clock	axat אחת
one fifteen	axat va'reva אחת ורבע
one thirty	axat va'xetsi אחת וחצי
one forty-five	axat arba'im vexameʃ אחת ארבעים וחמש
one | two | three	axat | ʃtayim | ʃaloʃ אחת | שתיים | שלוש
four | five | six	arba | xameʃ | ʃeʃ ארבע | חמש | שש
seven | eight | nine	ʃeva | ʃmone | 'teʃa שבע | שמונה | תשע
ten | eleven | twelve	eser | axat esre | ʃtem esre עשר | אחת עשרה | שתים עשרה
in …	tox … תוך ...
five minutes	xameʃ dakot חמש דקות
ten minutes	eser dakot עשר דקות
fifteen minutes	xameʃ esre dakot חמש עשרה דקות
twenty minutes	esrim dakot עשרים דקות
half an hour	xatsi ʃa'a חצי שעה
an hour	ʃa'a שעה

in the morning	ba'boker בבוקר
early in the morning	mukdam ba'boker, haʃkem ba'boker מוקדם בבוקר, השכם בבוקר
this morning	ha'boker הבוקר
tomorrow morning	maχar ba'boker מחר בבוקר
in the middle of the day	batsaha'rayim בצהריים
in the afternoon	aχar hatsaha'rayim אחר הצהריים
in the evening	ba''erev בערב
tonight	ha'laila הלילה
at night	ba'laila בלילה
yesterday	etmol אתמול
today	hayom היום
tomorrow	maχar מחר
the day after tomorrow	maχara'tayim מחרתיים
What day is it today?	eize yom hayom? איזה יום היום?
It's ...	hayom ... היום ...
Monday	yom ʃeni יום שני
Tuesday	yom ʃliʃi יום שלישי
Wednesday	yom revi'i יום רביעי
Thursday	yom χamiʃi יום חמישי
Friday	yom ʃiʃi יום ששי
Saturday	ʃabat שבת
Sunday	yom riʃon יום ראשון

Greetings. Introductions

Pleased to meet you. (man ⇨ man)
ani sameax lehakir otxa.
אני שמח להכיר אותך.

Pleased to meet you. (man ⇨ woman)
ani sameax lehakir otax.
אני שמח להכיר אותך.

Pleased to meet you. (woman ⇨ man)
ani smexa lifgoʃ otxa.
אני שמחה לפגוש אותך.

Pleased to meet you. (woman ⇨ woman)
ani smexa lifgoʃ otax.
אני שמחה לפגוש אותך.

Hello.
ʃalom.
שלום.

Me too.
gam ani.
גם אני.

I'd like you to meet ... (man ⇨ man)
ha'yiti rotse ʃetakir et ...
הייתי רוצה שתכיר את ...

I'd like you to meet ... (man ⇨ woman)
ha'yiti rotse ʃeta'kiri et ...
הייתי רוצה שתכירי את ...

I'd like you to meet ... (woman ⇨ man)
ha'yiti rotsa ʃetakir et ...
הייתי רוצה שתכיר את ...

I'd like you to meet ... (woman ⇨ woman)
ha'yiti rotsa ʃeta'kiri et ...
הייתי רוצה שתכירי את ...

Nice to meet you. (⇨ man)
na'im lifgoʃ otxa.
נעים לפגוש אותך.

Nice to meet you. (⇨ woman)
na'im lifgoʃ otax.
נעים לפגוש אותך.

How are you? (⇨ man)
ma ʃlomxa?
מה שלומך?

How are you? (⇨ woman)
ma ʃlomex?
מה שלומך?

My name is ...
kor'im li ...
קוראים לי ...

His name is ...
kor'im lo ...
קוראים לו ...

Her name is ...
kor'im la ...
קוראים לה ...

What's your name? (⇨ man)
eix kor'im lexa?
איך קוראים לך?

What's your name? (⇨ woman)
eix kor'im lax?
איך קוראים לך?

What's his name?
eix kor'im lo?
איך קוראים לו?

What's her name?
eix kor'im la?
איך קוראים לה?

What's your last name? (⇨ man)	ma ʃem hamiʃpaχa ʃelχa? מה שם המשפחה שלך?
What's your last name? (⇨ woman)	ma ʃem hamiʃpaχa ʃelaχ? מה שם המשפחה שלך?
You can call me ... (⇨ man)	ata yaχol likro li ... אתה יכול לקרוא לי ...
You can call me ... (⇨ woman)	at yeχola likro li ... את יכולה לקרוא לי ...
Where are you from? (⇨ man)	me"eifo ata? מאיפה אתה?
Where are you from? (⇨ woman)	me"eifo at? מאיפה את?

I'm from ...	ani mi... אני מ...
What do you do for a living? (⇨ man)	bema ata oved? במה אתה עובד?
What do you do for a living? (⇨ woman)	bema at o'vedet? במה את עובדת?

Who is this? (masc.)	mi ze? מי זה?
Who is this? (fem.)	mi zo? מי זו?
Who is he?	mi ze? מי זה?
Who is she?	mi zo? מי זו?
Who are they?	mi 'ele? מי אלה?

This is ...	ze ... זה ...
my friend (masc.)	χaver ʃeli חבר שלי
my husband	ba'ali בעלי
my father	avi אבי
my brother	aχi אחי
my son	bni בני

This is ...	zo ... זו ...
my friend (fem.)	χavera ʃeli חברה שלי
my wife	iʃti אשתי
my mother	immi אמי

my sister	aχoti
	אחותי
my daughter	biti
	בתי

This is our son.	ze haben ʃe'lanu.
	זה הבן שלנו.
This is our daughter.	zo habat ʃe'lanu.
	זו הבת שלנו.
These are my children.	ele hayeladim ʃeli.
	אלה הילדים שלי.
These are our children.	ele hayeladim ʃe'lanu.
	אלה הילדים שלנו.

Farewells

Good bye!	ʃalom! שלום!
Bye! (inform.)	bai! ביי!
See you tomorrow.	lehitra'ot maχar. להתראות מחר.
See you soon.	lehitra'ot bekarov. להתראות בקרוב.
See you at seven.	lehitra'ot be'ʃeva. להתראות בשבע.
Have fun!	asu χayim! עשו חיים!
Talk to you later.	lehiʃta'me'a. להשתמע.
Have a nice weekend.	sof ʃa'vu'a na'im. סוף שבוע נעים.
Good night.	laila tov. לילה טוב.
It's time for me to go.	hi'gi'a zmani la'leχet. הגיע זמני ללכת.
I have to go. (man ⇨)	ani χayav la'leχet. אני חייב ללכת.
I have to go. (woman ⇨)	ani χa'yevet la'leχet. אני חייבת ללכת.
I will be right back.	ani aχazor miyad. אני אחזור מייד.
It's late.	kvar me'uχar. כבר מאוחר.
I have to get up early. (man ⇨)	ani tsariχ lakum mukdam. אני צריך לקום מוקדם.
I have to get up early. (woman ⇨)	ani tsriχa lakum mukdam. אני צריכה לקום מוקדם.
I'm leaving tomorrow. (man ⇨)	ani ozev maχar. אני עוזב מחר.
I'm leaving tomorrow. (woman ⇨)	ani o'zevet maχar. אני עוזבת מחר.
We're leaving tomorrow. (couple , men ⇨)	a'naχnu ozvim maχar. אנחנו עוזבים מחר.
We're leaving tomorrow. (women ⇨)	a'naχnu ozvot maχar. אנחנו עוזבות מחר.

Have a nice trip!   nesi'a tova!
נסיעה טובה!

It was nice meeting you. (⇨ man)   haya neχmad lifgoʃ otχa.
היה נחמד לפגוש אותך.

It was nice meeting you. (⇨ woman)   haya neχmad lifgoʃ otaχ.
היה נחמד לפגוש אותך.

It was nice talking to you. (⇨ man)   haya na'im ledaber itχa.
היה נעים לדבר איתך.

It was nice talking to you. (⇨ woman)   haya na'im ledaber itaχ.
היה נעים לדבר איתך.

Thanks for everything.   toda al hakol.
תודה על הכל.

I had a very good time.   nehe'neti me'od.
נהניתי מאוד.

We had a very good time.   nehe'nenu me'od.
נהנינו מאוד.

It was really great.   ze haya mamaʃ nehedar.
זה היה ממש נהדר.

I'm going to miss you. (⇨ man)   ani etga'a'ge'a e'leχa.
אני אתגעגע אליך.

I'm going to miss you. (⇨ woman)   ani etga'a'ge'a e'layiχ.
אני אתגעגע אלייך.

We're going to miss you. (⇨ man)   a'naχnu nitga'a'ge'a e'leχa.
אנחנו נתגעגע אליך.

We're going to miss you. (⇨ woman)   a'naχnu nitga'a'ge'a e'layiχ.
אנחנו נתגעגע אלייך.

Good luck!   behatslaχa!
בהצלחה!

Say hi to … (⇨ man)   msor daʃ le…
מסור ד"ש ל...

Say hi to … (⇨ woman)   misri daʃ le…
מסרי ד"ש ל...

Foreign language

I don't understand. (man ⇨)	ani lo mevin. אני לא מבין.
I don't understand. (woman ⇨)	ani lo mevina. אני לא מבינה.
Write it down, please. (⇨ man)	ktov li et ze, bevakaʃa. כתוב לי את זה, בבקשה.
Write it down, please. (⇨ woman)	kitvi li et ze, bevakaʃa. כתבי לי את זה, בבקשה.
Do you speak ...? (⇨ man)	ha'im ata medaber ...? האם אתה מדבר ...?
Do you speak ...? (⇨ woman)	ha'im at meda'beret ...? האם את מדברת ...?
I speak a little bit of ... (man ⇨)	ani medaber ktsat ... אני מדבר קצת ...
I speak a little bit of ... (woman ⇨)	ani meda'beret ktsat ... אני מדברת קצת ...
English	anglit אנגלית
Turkish	turkit טורקית
Arabic	aravit ערבית
French	tsarfatit צרפתית
German	germanit גרמנית
Italian	italkit איטלקית
Spanish	sfaradit ספרדית
Portuguese	portu'gezit פורטוגזית
Chinese	sinit סינית
Japanese	ya'panit יפנית
Can you repeat that, please. (⇨ man)	ha'im ata yaχol laχazor al ze, bevakaʃa? האם אתה יכול לחזור על זה, בבקשה?
Can you repeat that, please. (⇨ woman)	ha'im at yeχola laχazor al ze, bevakaʃa? האם את יכולה לחזור על זה, בבקשה?

I understand. (man ⇨)	ani mevin. אני מבין.
I understand. (woman ⇨)	ani mevina. אני מבינה.
I don't understand. (man ⇨)	ani lo mevin. אני לא מבין.
I don't understand. (woman ⇨)	ani lo mevina. אני לא מבינה.
Please speak more slowly. (⇨ man)	ana daber yoter le'at. אנא דבר יותר לאט.
Please speak more slowly. (⇨ woman)	ana dabri yoter le'at. אנא דברי יותר לאט.

Is that correct? (Am I saying it right?)	ha'im ze naχon? האם זה נכון?
What is this? (What does this mean?)	ma ze? מה זה?

Apologies

Excuse me, please. (⇨ man)	slaχ li, bevakaʃa.
	סלח לי, בבקשה.
Excuse me, please. (⇨ woman)	silχi li, bevakaʃa.
	סלחי לי, בבקשה.
I'm sorry. (man ⇨)	ani mitsta'er.
	אני מצטער.
I'm sorry. (woman ⇨)	ani mitsta''eret.
	אני מצטערת.
I'm really sorry. (man ⇨)	ani mamaʃ mitsta'er.
	אני ממש מצטער.
I'm really sorry. (woman ⇨)	ani mamaʃ mitsta''eret.
	אני ממש מצטערת.
Sorry, it's my fault.	sliχa, zo aʃmati.
	סליחה, זו אשמתי.
My mistake.	ta'ut ʃeli.
	טעות שלי.

May I ...? (man ⇨)	ha'im ani yaχol ...?
	האם אני יכול ...?
May I ...? (woman ⇨)	ha'im ani yeχola ...?
	האם אני יכולה ...?
Do you mind if I ...? (⇨ man)	ha'im iχpat leχa im ani ...?
	האם איכפת לך אם אני ...?
Do you mind if I ...? (⇨ woman)	ha'im iχpat laχ im ani ...?
	האם איכפת לך אם אני ...?
It's OK.	ze be'seder.
	זה בסדר.
It's all right.	ze be'seder.
	זה בסדר.
Don't worry about it. (⇨ man)	al taχʃov al ze.
	אל תחשוב על זה.
Don't worry about it. (⇨ woman)	al taχʃevi al ze.
	אל תחשבי על זה.

Agreement

Yes.	ken.
	כן.
Yes, sure.	ken, bevadai.
	כן, בוודאי.
OK (Good!)	tov!
	טוב!
Very well.	be'seder gamur.
	בסדר גמור.
Certainly!	bevadai!
	בוודאי!
I agree. (man ⇨)	ani maskim.
	אני מסכים.
I agree. (woman ⇨)	ani maskima.
	אני מסכימה.
That's correct.	ze naχon.
	זה נכון.
That's right.	ze naχon.
	זה נכון.
You're right. (⇨ man)	ata tsodek.
	אתה צודק.
You're right. (⇨ woman)	at tso'deket.
	את צודקת.
I don't mind.	lo meʃane li.
	לא משנה לי.
Absolutely right.	naχon me'od.
	נכון מאוד.
It's possible.	yitaχen, ze efʃari.
	ייתכן, זה אפשרי.
That's a good idea.	ze ra'ayon tov.
	זה רעיון טוב.
I can't say no. (man ⇨)	ani lo yaχol lesarev.
	אני לא יכול לסרב.
I can't say no. (woman ⇨)	ani lo yeχola lesarev.
	אני לא יכולה לסרב.
I'd be happy to.	esmaχ la'asot et ze.
	אשמח לעשות את זה.
With pleasure.	bekef.
	בכיף.

Refusal. Expressing doubt

No.
lo.
לא.

Certainly not.
ba'tuaχ ʃelo.
בטוח שלא.

I don't agree. (man ⇨)
ani lo maskim.
אני לא מסכים.

I don't agree. (woman ⇨)
ani lo maskima.
אני לא מסכימה.

I don't think so. (man ⇨)
ani lo χoʃev kaχ.
אני לא חושב כך.

I don't think so. (woman ⇨)
ani lo χoʃevet kaχ.
אני לא חושבת כך.

It's not true.
ze lo naχon.
זה לא נבון.

You are wrong. (⇨ man)
ata to'e.
אתה טועה.

You are wrong. (⇨ woman)
at to'a.
את טועה.

I think you are wrong. (man ⇨ man)
ani χoʃev ʃe'ata to'e.
אני חושב שאתה טועה.

I think you are wrong. (man ⇨ woman)
ani χoʃev ʃe'at to'a.
אני חושב שאת טועה.

I think you are wrong. (woman ⇨ man)
ani χo'ʃevet ʃe'ata to'e.
אני חושבת שאתה טועה.

I think you are wrong. (woman ⇨ woman)
ani χo'ʃevet ʃe'at to'a.
אני חושבת שאת טועה.

I'm not sure. (man ⇨)
ani lo ba'tuaχ.
אני לא בטוח.

I'm not sure. (woman ⇨)
ani lo betuχa.
אני לא בטוחה.

It's impossible.
ze 'bilti efʃari.
זה בלתי אפשרי.

Nothing of the kind (sort)!
beʃum panim va''ofen lo!
בשום פנים ואופן לא!

The exact opposite.
bediyuk ha'hefeχ.
בדיוק ההיפך.

I'm against it. (man ⇨)
ani mitnaged leze.
אני מתנגד לזה.

I'm against it. (woman ⇨)
ani mitna'gedet leze.
אני מתנגדת לזה.

I don't care.
lo iχpat li.
לא איכפת לי.

I have no idea.	ein li musag.
	אין לי מושג.
I doubt it. (man ⇨)	ani lo ba'tuaχ.
	אני לא בטוח.
I doubt it. (woman ⇨)	ani lo betuχa.
	אני לא בטוחה.

Sorry, I can't. (man ⇨)	mitsta'er, ani lo yaχol.
	מצטער, אני לא יכול.
Sorry, I can't. (woman ⇨)	mitsta"eret, ani lo yeχola.
	מצטערת, אני לא יכולה.
Sorry, I don't want to. (man ⇨)	mitsta'er, ani lo me'unyan.
	מצטער, אני לא מעוניין.
Sorry, I don't want to. (woman ⇨)	mitsta"eret, ani lo me'un'yenet.
	מצטערת, אני לא מעוניינת.
Thank you, but I don't need this. (man ⇨)	toda, aval ani lo tsariχ et ze.
	תודה, אבל אני לא צריך את זה.
Thank you, but I don't need this. (woman ⇨)	toda, aval ani lo tsriχa et ze.
	תודה, אבל אני לא צריכה את זה.

It's getting late.	matχil lihyot me'uχar.
	מתחיל להיות מאוחר.
I have to get up early. (man ⇨)	ani tsariχ lakum mukdam.
	אני צריך לקום מוקדם.
I have to get up early. (woman ⇨)	ani tsriχa lakum mukdam.
	אני צריכה לקום מוקדם.
I don't feel well. (man ⇨)	ani lo margiʃ tov.
	אני לא מרגיש טוב.
I don't feel well. (woman ⇨)	ani lo margiʃa tov.
	אני לא מרגישה טוב.

Expressing gratitude

Thank you.	toda. תודה.
Thank you very much.	toda raba. תודה רבה.
I really appreciate it. (man ⇨)	ani be'emet ma'ariχ et ze. אני באמת מעריך את זה.
I really appreciate it. (woman ⇨)	ani be'emet ma'ariχa et ze. אני באמת מעריכה את זה.
I'm really grateful to you. (man ⇨ man)	ani mamaʃ asir toda leχa. אני ממש אסיר תודה לך.
I'm really grateful to you. (man ⇨ woman)	ani mamaʃ asir toda laχ. אני ממש אסיר תודה לך.
I'm really grateful to you. (woman ⇨ man)	ani mamaʃ asirat toda leχa. אני ממש אסירת תודה לך.
I'm really grateful to you. (woman ⇨ woman)	ani mamaʃ asirat toda laχ. אני ממש אסירת תודה לך.
Thank you for your time. (⇨ man)	toda al hazman ʃehik'daʃta. תודה על הזמן שהקדשת.
Thank you for your time. (⇨ woman)	toda al hazman ʃehikdaʃt. תודה על הזמן שהקדשת.
Thanks for everything.	toda al hakol. תודה על הכל.
Thank you for ...	toda al ... תודה על ...
your help (⇨ man)	ezratχa עזרתך
your help (⇨ woman)	ezrateχ עזרתך
a nice time	haχavaya hamehana החוויה המהנה
a wonderful meal	aruχa nehe'deret ארוחה נהדרת
a pleasant evening	erev na'im ערב נעים
a wonderful day	yom nifla יום נפלא
an amazing journey	tiyul madhim טיול מדהים
Don't mention it.	ein be'ad ma. אין בעד מה.
You are welcome.	bevakaʃa. בבקשה.

Any time.

ein be'ad ma.
אין בעד מה.

My pleasure.

ha"oneg kulo ʃeli.
העונג כולו שלי.

Forget it.

lo meʃane.
לא משנה.

Don't worry about it. (⇨ man)

al tid'ag.
אל תדאג.

Don't worry about it. (⇨ woman)

al tid'agi.
אל תדאגי.

Congratulations. Best wishes

Congratulations!	birχotai! ברכותיי!
Happy birthday!	mazal tov leyom hahu'ledet! מזל טוב ליום ההולדת!
Merry Christmas!	χag molad sa'meaχ! חג מולד שמח!
Happy New Year!	ʃana tova! שנה טובה!

Happy Easter!	χag pasχa sa'meaχ! חג פסחא שמח!
Happy Hanukkah!	χag 'χanuka sa'meaχ! חג חנוכה שמח!

I'd like to propose a toast. (man ⇨)	ani rotse leharim kosit. אני רוצה להרים כוסית.
I'd like to propose a toast. (woman ⇨)	ani rotsa leharim kosit. אני רוצה להרים כוסית.
Cheers!	le'χayim! לחיים!
Let's drink to ...!	bo'u niʃte le ...! בואו נשתה ל ...!
To our success!	lehatslaχa'tenu! להצלחתנו!
To your success! (⇨ man)	lehatslaχatχa! להצלחתך!
To your success! (⇨ woman)	lehatslaχateχ! להצלחתך!

Good luck!	behatslaχa! בהצלחה!
Have a nice day! (⇨ man)	ʃeyihye leχa yom na'im! שיהיה לך יום נעים!
Have a nice day! (⇨ woman)	ʃeyihye laχ yom na'im! שיהיה לך יום נעים!
Have a good holiday!	χufʃa ne'ima! חופשה נעימה!
Have a safe journey!	nesi'a tova! נסיעה טובה!
I hope you get better soon! (man ⇨ man)	ani mekave ʃetaχlim maher! אני מקווה שתחלים מהר!
I hope you get better soon! (man ⇨ woman)	ani mekave ʃetaχ'limi maher! אני מקווה שתחלימי מהר!

I hope you get better soon!
(woman ⇨ man)

ani mekava ʃetaχlim maher!
אני מקווה שתחלים מהר!

I hope you get better soon!
(woman ⇨ woman)

ani mekava ʃetaχ'limi maher!
אני מקווה שתחלימי מהר!

Socializing

Why are you sad? (⇨ man)	lama ata atsuv? ?למה אתה עצוב
Why are you sad? (⇨ woman)	lama at atsuva? ?למה את עצובה
Smile! Cheer up! (⇨ man)	χayeχ ktsat! !חייך קצת
Smile! Cheer up! (⇨ woman)	χaiχi ktsat! !חייכי קצת
Are you free tonight? (⇨ man)	ha'im ata panui ha''erev? ?האם אתה פנוי הערב
Are you free tonight? (⇨ woman)	ha'im at pnuya ha''erev? ?האם את פנויה הערב

May I offer you a drink?	ha'im efʃar leha'tsi'a laχ maʃke? ?האם אפשר להציע לך משקה
Would you like to dance? (⇨ man)	ha'im ata rotse lirkod? ?האם אתה רוצה לרקוד
Would you like to dance? (⇨ woman)	ha'im at rotsa lirkod? ?האם את רוצה לרקוד
Let's go to the movies. (⇨ man)	bo neleχ le'seret. .בוא נלך לסרט
Let's go to the movies. (⇨ woman)	bo'i neleχ le'seret. .בואי נלך לסרט

May I invite you to ...?	ha'im efʃar lehazmin otaχ le ...? ?... האם אפשר להזמין אותך ל
a restaurant	mis'ada מסעדה
the movies	seret סרט
the theater	te'atron תיאטרון
go for a walk	letiyul ba'regel לטיול ברגל

At what time?	be''eizo ʃa'a? ?באיזו שעה
tonight	ha'laila הלילה
at six	beʃeʃ בשש
at seven	be'ʃeva בשבע

at eight	biˈʃmone
	בשמונה
at nine	beˈteʃa
	בתשע

Do you like it here? (⇨ man)	ha'im hamakom motse χen be'ei'neχa?
	האם המקום מוצא חן בעיניך?
Do you like it here? (⇨ woman)	ha'im hamakom motse χen be'ei'nayiχ?
	האם המקום מוצא חן בעינייך?
Are you here with someone? (⇨ man)	ha'im ata nimtsa kan im 'miʃehu?
	האם אתה נמצא כאן עם מישהו?
Are you here with someone? (⇨ woman)	ha'im at nimtset kan im 'miʃehu?
	האם את נמצאת כאן עם מישהו?
I'm with my friend.	ani kan im χaver /χavera/.
	אני כאן עם חבר /חברה/.
I'm with my friends.	ani kan im χaverim.
	אני כאן עם חברים.
No, I'm alone.	lo, ani levad.
	לא, אני לבד.
Do you have a boyfriend?	ha'im yeʃ laχ χaver?
	האם יש לך חבר?
I have a boyfriend.	yeʃ li χaver.
	יש לי חבר.
Do you have a girlfriend?	ha'im yeʃ leχa χavera?
	האם יש לך חברה?
I have a girlfriend.	yeʃ li χavera.
	יש לי חברה.

Can I see you again? (⇨ man)	ha'im tirtse lehipageʃ ʃuv?
	האם תרצה להיפגש שוב?
Can I see you again? (⇨ woman)	ha'im tirtsi lehipageʃ ʃuv?
	האם תרצי להיפגש שוב?
Can I call you? (man ⇨ man)	ha'im ani yaχol lehitkaʃer e'leχa?
	האם אני יכול להתקשר אליך?
Can I call you? (man ⇨ woman)	ha'im ani yaχol lehitkaʃer e'layiχ?
	האם אני יכול להתקשר אלייך?
Can I call you? (woman ⇨ man)	ha'im ani yeχola lehitkaʃer e'leχa?
	האם אני יכולה להתקשר אליך?
Can I call you? (woman ⇨ woman)	ha'im ani yeχola lehitkaʃer e'layiχ?
	האם אני יכולה להתקשר אלייך?
Call me. (Give me a call.) (⇨ man)	hitkaʃer elai.
	התקשר אליי.
Call me. (Give me a call.) (⇨ woman)	hitkaʃri elai.
	התקשרי אליי.
What's your number? (⇨ man)	ma hamispar ʃelχa?
	מה המספר שלך?
What's your number? (⇨ woman)	ma hamispar ʃelaχ?
	מה המספר שלך?
I miss you. (man ⇨ man)	ani mitga'a"ge'a e'leχa.
	אני מתגעגע אליך.
I miss you. (man ⇨ woman)	ani mitga'a"ge'a e'layiχ.
	אני מתגעגע אלייך.

I miss you. (woman ⇨ man)	ani mitga'a''ga'at e'leχa.
	אני מתגעגעת אליך.
I miss you. (woman ⇨ woman)	ani mitga'a''ga'at e'layiχ.
	אני מתגעגעת אלייך.

You have a beautiful name. (man ⇨ man)	yeʃ leχa ʃem maksim.
	יש לך שם מקסים.
You have a beautiful name. (man ⇨ woman)	yeʃ laχ ʃem maksim.
	יש לך שם מקסים.
I love you.	ani ohev otaχ.
	אני אוהב אותך.
Will you marry me?	ha'im titχatni iti?
	האם תתחתני איתי?
You're kidding!	at tso'χeket alai!
	את צוחקת עליי!
I'm just kidding. (man ⇨)	ani stam mitba'deaχ.
	אני סתם מתבדח.
I'm just kidding. (woman ⇨)	ani stam mitba'daχat.
	אני סתם מתבדחת.

Are you serious? (⇨ man)	ha'im ata retsini?
	האם אתה רציני?
Are you serious? (⇨ woman)	ha'im at retsinit?
	האם את רצינית?
I'm serious. (man ⇨)	ani retsini.
	אני רציני.
I'm serious. (woman ⇨)	ani retsinit.
	אני רצינית.
Really?!	be'emet?!
	באמת?!

It's unbelievable!	ze lo ye'uman!
	זה לא יאומן!
I don't believe you. (man ⇨ man)	ani lo ma'amin leχa.
	אני לא מאמין לך.
I don't believe you. (man ⇨ woman)	ani lo ma'amin laχ.
	אני לא מאמין לך.
I don't believe you. (woman ⇨ man)	ani lo ma'amina leχa.
	אני לא מאמינה לך.
I don't believe you. (woman ⇨ woman)	ani lo ma'amina laχ.
	אני לא מאמינה לך.

I can't. (man ⇨)	ani lo yaχol.
	אני לא יכול.
I can't. (woman ⇨)	ani lo yeχola.
	אני לא יכולה.
I don't know. (man ⇨)	ani lo yo'de'a.
	אני לא יודע.
I don't know. (woman ⇨)	ani lo yo'da'at.
	אני לא יודעת.
I don't understand you. (man ⇨ man)	ani lo mevin otχa.
	אני לא מבין אותך.

I don't understand you. (man ⇨ woman)   ani lo mevin otaχ
אני לא מבין אותך.

I don't understand you. (woman ⇨ man)   ani lo mevina otχa.
אני לא מבינה אותך.

I don't understand you. (woman ⇨ woman)   ani lo mevina otaχ.
אני לא מבינה אותך.

Please go away. (⇨ man)   leχ mipo bevakaʃa.
לך מפה בבקשה.

Please go away. (⇨ woman)   leχi mipo bevakaʃa.
לכי מפה בבקשה.

Leave me alone! (⇨ man)   azov oti!
עזוב אותי!

Leave me alone! (⇨ woman)   izvi oti!
עזבי אותי!

I can't stand him. (man ⇨)   ani lo sovel oto.
אני לא סובל אותו.

I can't stand him. (woman ⇨)   ani lo so'velet oto.
אני לא סובלת אותו.

You are disgusting! (⇨ man)   ata mag'il!
אתה מגעיל!

You are disgusting! (⇨ woman)   at mag'ila!
את מגעילה!

I'll call the police!   ani azmin miʃtara!
אני אזמין משטרה!

Sharing impressions. Emotions

I like it.	ze moťse χen be'einai. זה מוצא חן בעיניי.
Very nice.	neχmad me'od. נחמד מאוד.
That's great!	ze nehedar! זה נהדר!
It's not bad.	ze lo ra. זה לא רע.

I don't like it.	ze lo moťse χen be'einai. זה לא מוצא חן בעיניי.
It's not good.	ze lo yafe. זה לא יפה.
It's bad.	ze ra. זה רע.
It's very bad.	ze ra me'od. זה רע מאוד.
It's disgusting.	ze mag'il. זה מגעיל.

I'm happy. (man ⇨)	ani me'uʃar. אני מאושר.
I'm happy. (woman ⇨)	ani me'u'ʃeret. אני מאושרת.
I'm content. (man ⇨)	ani meruťse. אני מרוצה.
I'm content. (woman ⇨)	ani meruťsa. אני מרוצה.
I'm in love. (man ⇨)	ani me'ohav. אני מאוהב.
I'm in love. (woman ⇨)	ani me'o'hevet. אני מאוהבת.
I'm calm. (man ⇨)	ani ra'gu'a. אני רגוע.
I'm calm. (woman ⇨)	ani regu'a. אני רגועה.
I'm bored. (man ⇨)	ani meʃu'amam. אני משועמם.
I'm bored. (woman ⇨)	ani meʃu'a'memet. אני משועממת.
I'm tired. (man ⇨)	ani ayef. אני עייף.
I'm tired. (woman ⇨)	ani ayefa. אני עייפה.

I'm sad. (man ⇨)

ani atsuv.
אני עצוב.

I'm sad. (woman ⇨)

ani atsuva.
אני עצובה.

I'm frightened. (man ⇨)

ani poxed.
אני פוחד.

I'm frightened. (woman ⇨)

ani po'xedet.
אני פוחדת.

I'm angry. (man ⇨)

ani ko'es.
אני כועס.

I'm angry. (woman ⇨)

ani ko''eset.
אני כועסת.

I'm worried. (man ⇨)

ani mud'ag.
אני מודאג.

I'm worried. (woman ⇨)

ani mud''eget.
אני מודאגת.

I'm nervous. (man ⇨)

ani atsbani.
אני עצבני.

I'm nervous. (woman ⇨)

ani atsbanit.
אני עצבנית.

I'm jealous. (envious) (man ⇨)

ani mekane.
אני מקנא.

I'm jealous. (envious) (woman ⇨)

ani mekanet.
אני מקנאת.

I'm surprised. (man ⇨)

ani mufta.
אני מופתע.

I'm surprised. (woman ⇨)

ani muf'ta'at.
אני מופתעת.

I'm perplexed. (man ⇨)

ani mevulbal.
אני מבולבל.

I'm perplexed. (woman ⇨)

ani mevul'belet.
אני מבולבלת.

Problems. Accidents

I've got a problem.	yeʃ li be'aya.
	יש לי בעייה.
We've got a problem.	yeʃ 'lanu be'aya.
	יש לנו בעייה.
I'm lost.	ha'laχti le'ibud.
	הלכתי לאיבוד.
I missed the last bus.	fis'fasti et ha''otobus ha'aχaron.
	פספסתי את האוטובוס האחרון.
I missed the last train.	fis'fasti et hara'kevet ha'aχrona.
	פספסתי את הרכבת האחרונה.
I don't have any money left.	niʃ''arti bli 'kesef.
	נשארתי בלי כסף.

I've lost my …	i'badti et ha… ʃeli
	איבדתי את ה... שלי
Someone stole my …	miʃehu ganav et ha… ʃeli
	מישהו גנב את ה... שלי
passport	darkon
	דרכון
wallet	arnak
	ארנק
papers	te'udot
	תעודות
ticket	kartis
	כרטיס

money	kesef
	כסף
handbag	tik yad
	תיק יד
camera	matslema
	מצלמה
laptop	maχʃev nayad
	מחשב נייד
tablet computer	maχʃev ʃulχani
	מחשב שולחני
mobile phone	telefon nayad
	טלפון נייד

Help me!	izru li!
	עזרו לי!
What's happened?	ma kara?
	מה קרה?

fire	srefa
	שרפה
shooting	yeriyot
	יריות
murder	retsax
	רצח
explosion	pitsuts
	פיצוץ
fight	ktata
	קטטה

Call the police!	haz'minu miʃtara
	הזמינו משטרה!
Please hurry up!	ana maharu!
	אנא מהרו!
I'm looking for the police station. (man ⇨)	ani mexapes et taxanat hamiʃtara.
	אני מחפש את תחנת המשטרה.
I'm looking for the police station. (woman ⇨)	ani mexa'peset et taxanat hamiʃtara.
	אני מחפשת את תחנת המשטרה.
I need to make a call. (man ⇨)	ani tsarix lehitkaʃer.
	אני צריך להתקשר.
I need to make a call. (woman ⇨)	ani tsrixa lehitkaʃer.
	אני צריכה להתקשר.
May I use your phone? (⇨ man)	ha'im eʃʃar lehiʃtameʃ be'telefon ʃelxa?
	האם אפשר להשתמש בטלפון שלך?
May I use your phone? (⇨ woman)	ha'im eʃʃar lehiʃtameʃ be'telefon ʃelax?
	האם אפשר להשתמש בטלפון שלך?

I've been …	ani …
	אני ...
mugged	hut'kafti
	הותקפתי
robbed	niʃ'dadti
	נשדדתי
raped	ne'e'nasti
	נאנסתי
attacked (beaten up)	hu'keti
	הוכיתי

Are you all right? (⇨ man)	ha'im ata be'seder?
	האם אתה בסדר?
Are you all right? (⇨ woman)	ha'im at be'seder?
	האם את בסדר?
Did you see who it was? (⇨ man)	ha'im ra''ita mi asa et ze?
	האם ראית מי עשה את זה?
Did you see who it was? (⇨ woman)	ha'im ra'it mi asa et ze?
	האם ראית מי עשה את זה?
Would you be able to recognize the person? (⇨ man)	ha'im tuxal lezahot et oto adam?
	האם תוכל לזהות את אותו אדם?
Would you be able to recognize the person? (⇨ woman)	ha'im tuxli lezahot et oto adam?
	האם תוכלי לזהות את אותו אדם?

Are you sure? (⇨ man)	ha'im ata ba'tuaχ? האם אתה בטוח?
Are you sure? (⇨ woman)	ha'im at betuχa? האם את בטוחה?

Please calm down. (⇨ man)	heraga, bevakaʃa. הירגע בבקשה.
Please calm down. (⇨ woman)	herag'i, bevakaʃa. הירגעי בבקשה.
Take it easy! (⇨ man)	teraga! תירגע!
Take it easy! (⇨ woman)	terag'i! תירגעי!
Don't worry! (⇨ man)	al tid'ag! אל תדאג!
Don't worry! (⇨ woman)	al tid'agi! אל תדאגי!
Everything will be fine.	hakol yihye be'seder. הכל יהיה בסדר.
Everything's all right.	hakol be'seder. הכל בסדר.

Come here, please. (⇨ man)	bo 'hena, bevakaʃa. בוא הנה, בבקשה.
Come here, please. (⇨ woman)	bo'i 'hena, bevakaʃa. בואי הנה, בבקשה.
I have some questions for you. (⇨ man)	yeʃ li 'kama ʃe'elot e'leχa. יש לי כמה שאלות אליך.
I have some questions for you. (⇨ woman)	yeʃ li 'kama ʃe'elot e'layiχ. יש לי כמה שאלות אלייך.
Wait a moment, please. (⇨ man)	χake 'rega, bevakaʃa. חכה רגע, בבקשה.
Wait a moment, please. (⇨ woman)	χaki 'rega, bevakaʃa. חכי רגע, בבקשה.
Do you have any I.D.? (⇨ man)	ha'im yeʃ leχa te'uda mezaha? האם יש לך תעודה מזהה?
Do you have any I.D.? (⇨ woman)	ha'im yeʃ laχ te'uda mezaha? האם יש לך תעודה מזהה?
Thanks. You can leave now. (⇨ man)	toda. ata yaχol la'leχet aχʃav. תודה. אתה יכול ללכת עכשיו.
Thanks. You can leave now. (⇨ woman)	toda. at yeχola la'leχet aχʃav. תודה. את יכולה ללכת עכשיו.
Hands behind your head!	ya'dayim aχarei haroʃ! ידיים אחרי הראש!
You're under arrest! (⇨ man)	ata atsur! אתה עצור!
You're under arrest! (⇨ woman)	at atsura! את עצורה!

Health problems

Please help me. (⇨ man)	azor li bevakaʃa. עזור לי בבקשה.
Please help me. (⇨ woman)	izri li bevakaʃa. עזרי לי בבקשה.
I don't feel well. (man ⇨)	ani lo margiʃ tov. אני לא מרגיש טוב.
I don't feel well. (woman ⇨)	ani lo margiʃa tov. אני לא מרגישה טוב.

My husband doesn't feel well.	ba'ali lo margiʃ tov. בעלי לא מרגיש טוב.
My son ...	haben ʃeli ... הבן שלי ...
My father ...	avi ... אבי ...

My wife doesn't feel well.	iʃti lo margiʃa tov. אשתי לא מרגישה טוב.
My daughter ...	habat ʃeli ... הבת שלי ...
My mother ...	immi ... אמי ...

I've got a ...	yeʃ li ... יש לי ...
headache	ke'ev roʃ כאב ראש
sore throat	ke'ev garon כאב גרון
stomach ache	ke'ev 'beten כאב בטן
toothache	ke'ev ʃi'nayim כאב שיניים

I feel dizzy.	yeʃ li sxar'xoret. יש לי סחרחורת.
He has a fever.	yeʃ lo xom. יש לו חום.
She has a fever.	yeʃ la xom. יש לה חום.
I can't breathe. (man ⇨)	ani lo yaxol linʃom. אני לא יכול לנשום.
I can't breathe. (woman ⇨)	ani lo yexola linʃom. אני לא יכולה לנשום.

I'm short of breath.	yeʃ li 'koʦer neʃima.
	יש לי קוצר נשימה.
I am asthmatic. (man ⇨)	ani ast'mati.
	אני אסתמתי.
I am asthmatic. (woman ⇨)	ani ast'matit.
	אני אסתמתית.
I am diabetic.	yeʃ li su'keret.
	יש לי סוכרת.
I can't sleep. (man ⇨)	ani lo yaχol liʃon.
	אני לא יכול לישון.
I can't sleep. (woman ⇨)	ani lo yeχola liʃon.
	אני לא יכולה לישון.
food poisoning	har'alat mazon
	הרעלת מזון

It hurts here.	ko'ev li kan.
	כואב לי כאן.
Help me!	izru li!
	עזרו לי!
I am here!	ani po!
	אני פה!
We are here!	a'naχnu kan!
	אנחנו כאן!
Get me out of here!	hoʦ'i'u oti mikan!
	הוציאו אותי מכאן!
I need a doctor. (man ⇨)	ani ʦariχ rofe.
	אני צריך רופא.
I need a doctor. (woman ⇨)	ani ʦriχa rofe.
	אני צריכה רופא.
I can't move. (man ⇨)	ani lo yaχol lazuz.
	אני לא יכול לזוז.
I can't move. (woman ⇨)	ani lo yeχola lazuz.
	אני לא יכולה לזוז.
I can't move my legs. (man ⇨)	ani lo yaχol lehaziz et harag'layim.
	אני לא יכול להזיז את הרגליים.
I can't move my legs. (woman ⇨)	ani lo yeχola lehaziz et harag'layim.
	אני לא יכולה להזיז את הרגליים.

I have a wound.	yeʃ li 'peʦa.
	יש לי פצע.
Is it serious?	ha'im ze reʦini?
	האם זה רציני?
My documents are in my pocket.	hate'udot ʃeli bakis.
	התעודות שלי בכיס.
Calm down! (⇨ man)	heraga!
	הירגע!
Calm down! (⇨ woman)	herag'i!
	הירגעי!
May I use your phone? (man ⇨ man)	ha'im ani yaχol lehiʃtameʃ ba'telefon ʃelχa?
	האם אני יכול להשתמש בטלפון שלך?

May I use your phone? (man ⇒ woman)	ha'im ani yaxol lehiʃtameʃ ba'telefon ʃelax? **האם אני יכול להשתמש בטלפון שלך?**
May I use your phone? (woman ⇒ woman)	ha'im ani yexola lehiʃtameʃ ba'telefon ʃelax? **האם אני יכולה להשתמש בטלפון שלך?**
May I use your phone? (woman ⇒ man)	ha'im ani yexola lehiʃtameʃ ba'telefon ʃelxa? **האם אני יכולה להשתמש בטלפון שלך?**

Call an ambulance!	haz'minu 'ambulans! **הזמינו אמבולנס!**
It's urgent!	ze daxuf! **זה דחוף!**
It's an emergency!	ze maʦav xerum! **זה מצב חירום!**
Please hurry up!	ana maharu! **אנא מהרו!**
Would you please call a doctor? (⇒ man)	ha'im ata yaxol lehazmin rofe, bevakaʃa? **האם אתה יכול להזמין רופא בבקשה?**
Would you please call a doctor? (⇒ woman)	ha'im at yexola lehazmin rofe, bevakaʃa? **האם את יכולה להזמין רופא בבקשה?**
Where is the hospital?	eifo beit haxolim? **איפה בית החולים?**

How are you feeling? (⇒ man)	eix ata margiʃ? **איך אתה מרגיש?**
How are you feeling? (⇒ woman)	eix at margiʃa? **איך את מרגישה?**
Are you all right? (⇒ man)	ha'im ata be'seder? **האם אתה בסדר?**
Are you all right? (⇒ woman)	ha'im at be'seder? **האם את בסדר?**
What's happened?	ma kara? **מה קרה?**
I feel better now. (man ⇒)	ani margiʃ yoter tov axʃav. **אני מרגיש טוב יותר עכשיו.**
I feel better now. (woman ⇒)	ani margiʃa yoter tov axʃav. **אני מרגישה טוב יותר עכשיו.**
It's OK.	ze be'seder. **זה בסדר.**
It's all right.	ze be'seder. **זה בסדר.**

At the pharmacy

pharmacy (drugstore)	beit mer'kaxat בית מרקחת
24-hour pharmacy	beit mer'kaxat pa'tuax esrim ve'arba ʃa'ot biymama בית מרקחת פתוח עשרים וארבע שעות ביממה
Where is the closest pharmacy?	eifo beit hamer'kaxat hakarov beyoter? איפה בית המרקחת הקרוב ביותר?
Is it open now?	ha'im ze pa'tuax axʃav? האם זה פתוח עכשיו?
At what time does it open?	be"eizo ʃa'a ze niftax? באיזו שעה זה נפתח?
At what time does it close?	be"eizo ʃa'a ze nisgar? באיזו שעה זה נסגר?
Is it far?	ha'im ze raxok? האם זה רחוק?
Can I get there on foot? (man ⇨)	ha'im ani yaxol la'lexet leʃam ba'regel? האם אני יכול ללכת לשם ברגל?
Can I get there on foot? (woman ⇨)	ha'im ani yexola la'lexet leʃam ba'regel? האם אני יכולה ללכת לשם ברגל?
Can you show me on the map? (⇨ man)	ha'im ata yaxol lehar'ot li al hamapa? האם אתה יכול להראות לי על המפה?
Can you show me on the map? (⇨ woman)	ha'im at yexola lehar'ot li al hamapa? האם את יכולה להראות לי על המפה?
Please give me something for ... (⇨ man)	ten li bevakaʃa 'maʃehu 'neged ... תן לי בבקשה משהו נגד ...
Please give me something for ... (⇨ woman)	tni li bevakaʃa 'maʃehu 'neged ... תני לי בבקשה משהו נגד ...
a headache	ke'ev roʃ כאב ראש
a cough	ʃi'ul שיעול
a cold	hitkarerut התקררות
the flu	ʃa'pa'at שפעת
a fever	xom חום
a stomach ache	ke'ev 'beten כאב בטן

nausea	bχila בחילה
diarrhea	ʃilʃul שלשול
constipation	atsirut עצירות
pain in the back	ke'ev bagav כאב בגב
chest pain	ke'ev baχaze כאב בחזה
side stitch	dkirot batsad דקירות בצד
abdominal pain	ke'ev ba'beten כאב בבטן
pill	glula גלולה
ointment, cream	miʃχa, krem משחה, קרם
syrup	sirop סירופ
spray	tarsis תרסיס
drops	tipot טיפות
You need to go to the hospital. (⇨ man)	ata tsariχ la'leχet leveit χolim. אתה צריך ללכת לבית חולים.
You need to go to the hospital. (⇨ woman)	at tsriχa la'leχet leveit χolim. את צריכה ללכת לבית חולים.
health insurance	bi'tuaχ bri'ut ביטוח בריאות
prescription	mirʃam מרשם
insect repellant	doχe χarakim דוחה חרקים
Band Aid	plaster פלסטר

The bare minimum

Excuse me, ... (⇨ man)	slaχ li, ... סלח לי, ...
Excuse me, ... (⇨ woman)	silχi li, ... סלחי לי, ...
Hello.	ʃalom. שלום.
Thank you.	toda. תודה.
Good bye.	lehitra'ot. להתראות.
Yes.	ken. כן.
No.	lo. לא.
I don't know. (man ⇨)	ani lo yo'de'a. אני לא יודע.
I don't know. (woman ⇨)	ani lo yo'da'at. אני לא יודעת.
Where?	Where to?	When?	eifo?	le'an?	matai? איפה?	לאן?	מתי?
I need ... (man ⇨)	ani tsariχ ... אני צריך ...
I need ... (woman ⇨)	ani tsriχa ... אני צריכה ...
I want ... (man ⇨)	ani rotse ... אני רוצה ...
I want ... (woman ⇨)	ani rotsa ... אני רוצה ...
Do you have ...? (⇨ man)	ha'im yeʃ leχa ...? האם יש לך ...?
Do you have ...? (⇨ woman)	ha'im yeʃ laχ ...? האם יש לך ...?
Is there a ... here?	ha'im yeʃ po ...? האם יש פה ...?
May I ...? (man ⇨)	ha'im ani yaχol ...? האם אני יבול ...?
May I ...? (woman ⇨)	ha'im ani yeχola ...? האם אני יבולה ...?
..., please (polite request)	..., bevakaʃa ..., בבקשה

I'm looking for ... (man ⇨)	ani meχapes ... אני מחפש ...
I'm looking for ... (woman ⇨)	ani meχa'peset ... אני מחפשת ...
the restroom	ʃerutim שירותים
an ATM	kaspomat כספומט
a pharmacy (drugstore)	beit mer'kaχat בית מרקחת
a hospital	beit χolim בית חולים
the police station	taχanat miʃtara תחנת משטרה
the subway	ra'kevet taχtit רכבת תחתית
a taxi	monit, 'teksi מונית, טקסי
the train station	taχanat ra'kevet תחנת רכבת

My name is ...	kor'im li ... קוראים לי ...
What's your name? (⇨ man)	eiχ kor'im leχa? איך קוראים לך?
What's your name? (⇨ woman)	eiχ kor'im laχ? איך קוראים לך?
Could you please help me? (⇨ man)	ha'im ata yaχol la'azor li? האם אתה יכול לעזור לי?
Could you please help me? (⇨ woman)	ha'im at yeχola la'azor li? האם את יכולה לעזור לי?
I've got a problem.	yeʃ li be'aya. יש לי בעייה.
I don't feel well. (man ⇨)	ani lo margiʃ tov. אני לא מרגיש טוב.
I don't feel well. (woman ⇨)	ani lo margiʃa tov. אני לא מרגישה טוב.
Call an ambulance! (⇨ man)	hazmen 'ambulans! הזמן אמבולנס!
Call an ambulance! (⇨ woman)	haz'mini 'ambulans! הזמיני אמבולנס!
May I make a call? (man ⇨)	ha'im ani yaχol lehitkaʃer? האם אני יכול להתקשר?
May I make a call? (woman ⇨)	ha'im ani yeχola lehitkaʃer? האם אני יכולה להתקשר?

I'm sorry. (man ⇨)	ani mitsta'er. אני מצטער.
I'm sorry. (woman ⇨)	ani mitsta''eret. אני מצטערת.
You're welcome.	ein be'ad ma, bevakaʃa. אין בעד מה, בבקשה.

I, me	ani אני
you (inform.) (masc.)	ata אתה
you (inform.) (fem.)	at את
he	hu הוא
she	hi היא
they (masc.)	hem הם
they (fem.)	hen הן
we	a'naxnu אנחנו
you (pl) (masc.)	atem אתם
you (pl) (fem.)	aten אתן
you (sg, form.) (masc.)	ata אתה
you (sg, form.) (fem.)	at את

ENTRANCE	knisa כניסה
EXIT	yetsi'a יציאה
OUT OF ORDER	lo po'el לא פועל
CLOSED	sagur סגור
OPEN	pa'tuax פתוח
FOR WOMEN	lenaʃim לנשים
FOR MEN	ligvarim לגברים

CONCISE DICTIONARY

This section contains more than 1,500 useful words arranged alphabetically. The dictionary includes a lot of gastronomic terms and will be helpful when ordering food at a restaurant or buying groceries

T&P Books Publishing

DICTIONARY CONTENTS

T&P Books Publishing

time	zman	זְמַן (ז)
hour	ʃa'a	שָׁעָה (נ)
half an hour	χatsi ʃa'a	חֲצִי שָׁעָה (נ)
minute	daka	דַקָה (נ)
second	ʃniya	שְׁנִייָה (נ)
today (adv)	hayom	הַיוֹם
tomorrow (adv)	maχar	מָחָר
yesterday (adv)	etmol	אֶתמוֹל
Monday	yom ʃeni	יוֹם שֵׁנִי (ז)
Tuesday	yom ʃliʃi	יוֹם שְׁלִישִׁי (ז)
Wednesday	yom revi'i	יוֹם רְבִיעִי (ז)
Thursday	yom χamiʃi	יוֹם חֲמִישִׁי (ז)
Friday	yom ʃiʃi	יוֹם שִׁישִׁי (ז)
Saturday	ʃabat	שַׁבָּת (נ)
Sunday	yom riʃon	יוֹם רִאשׁוֹן (ז)
day	yom	יוֹם (ז)
working day	yom avoda	יוֹם עֲבוֹדָה (ז)
public holiday	yom χag	יוֹם חַג (ז)
weekend	sof ʃa'vu'a	סוֹף שָׁבוּעַ
week	ʃa'vua	שָׁבוּעַ (ז)
last week (adv)	baʃa'vu'a ʃe'avar	בַּשָּׁבוּעַ שֶׁעָבַר
next week (adv)	baʃa'vu'a haba	בַּשָּׁבוּעַ הַבָּא
sunrise	zriχa	זְרִיחָה (נ)
sunset	ʃki'a	שְׁקִיעָה (נ)
in the morning	ba'boker	בַּבּוֹקֶר
in the afternoon	aχar hatsaha'rayim	אַחַר הַצָהֳרַיִים
in the evening	ba''erev	בָּעֶרֶב
tonight (this evening)	ha''erev	הָעֶרֶב
at night	ba'laila	בַּלַילָה
midnight	χatsot	חֲצוֹת (נ)
January	'yanu'ar	יָנוּאָר (ז)
February	'febru'ar	פֶבּרוּאָר (ז)
March	merts	מֶרץ (ז)
April	april	אַפּרִיל (ז)
May	mai	מַאי (ז)
June	'yuni	יוּנִי (ז)

July	'yuli	יוּלִי (ז)
August	'ogust	אוֹגוּסט (ז)
September	sep'tember	סֶפְּטֶמְבֶּר (ז)
October	ok'tober	אוֹקְטוֹבֶּר (ז)
November	no'vember	נוֹבֶמְבֶּר (ז)
December	de'tsember	דֶצֶמְבֶּר (ז)
in spring	ba'aviv	בָּאָבִיב
in summer	ba'kayits	בַּקַיִץ
in fall	bestav	בְּסְתָיו
in winter	ba'xoref	בַּחוֹרֶף
month	'xodeʃ	חוֹדֶש (ז)
season (summer, etc.)	ona	עוֹנָה (נ)
year	ʃana	שָׁנָה (נ)
century	'me'a	מֵאָה (נ)

2. Numbers. Numerals

digit, figure	sifra	סִפְרָה (נ)
number	mispar	מִסְפָּר (ז)
minus sign	'minus	מִינוּס (ז)
plus sign	plus	פְּלוּס (ז)
sum, total	sxum	סְכוּם (ז)
first (adj)	riʃon	רָאשׁוֹן
second (adj)	ʃeni	שֵׁנִי
third (adj)	ʃliʃi	שְׁלִישִׁי
0 zero	'efes	אֶפֶס (ז)
1 one	exad	אֶחָד (ז)
2 two	'ʃtayim	שְׁתַּיִם (נ)
3 three	ʃaloʃ	שָׁלוֹשׁ (נ)
4 four	arba	אַרְבַּע (נ)
5 five	xameʃ	חָמֵשׁ (נ)
6 six	ʃeʃ	שֵׁשׁ (נ)
7 seven	'ʃeva	שֶׁבַע (נ)
8 eight	'ʃmone	שְׁמוֹנֶה (נ)
9 nine	'teʃa	תֵּשַׁע (נ)
10 ten	'eser	עֶשֶׂר (נ)
11 eleven	axat esre	אַחַת־עֶשְׂרֵה (נ)
12 twelve	ʃteim esre	שְׁתֵּים־עֶשְׂרֵה (נ)
13 thirteen	ʃloʃ esre	שְׁלוֹשׁ־עֶשְׂרֵה (נ)
14 fourteen	arba esre	אַרְבַּע־עֶשְׂרֵה (נ)
15 fifteen	xameʃ esre	חָמֵשׁ־עֶשְׂרֵה (נ)
16 sixteen	ʃeʃ esre	שֵׁשׁ־עֶשְׂרֵה (נ)
17 seventeen	ʃva esre	שְׁבַע־עֶשְׂרֵה (נ)

18 eighteen	ʃmone esre	(נ) שְׁמוֹנֶה-עֶשְׂרֵה
19 nineteen	tʃa esre	(נ) תְּשַׁע-עֶשְׂרֵה
20 twenty	esrim	עֶשְׂרִים
30 thirty	ʃloʃim	שְׁלוֹשִׁים
40 forty	arba'im	אַרְבָּעִים
50 fifty	χamiʃim	חֲמִישִׁים
60 sixty	ʃiʃim	שִׁישִׁים
70 seventy	ʃiv'im	שִׁבְעִים
80 eighty	ʃmonim	שְׁמוֹנִים
90 ninety	tiʃim	תִּשְׁעִים
100 one hundred	'me'a	(נ) מֵאָה
200 two hundred	ma'tayim	מָאתַיִם
300 three hundred	ʃloʃ me'ot	(נ) שְׁלוֹשׁ מֵאוֹת
400 four hundred	arba me'ot	(נ) אַרְבַּע מֵאוֹת
500 five hundred	χameʃ me'ot	(נ) חֲמֵשׁ מֵאוֹת
600 six hundred	ʃeʃ me'ot	(נ) שֵׁשׁ מֵאוֹת
700 seven hundred	ʃva me'ot	(נ) שְׁבַע מֵאוֹת
800 eight hundred	ʃmone me'ot	(נ) שְׁמוֹנֶה מֵאוֹת
900 nine hundred	tʃa me'ot	(נ) תְּשַׁע מֵאוֹת
1000 one thousand	'elef	(ז) אֶלֶף
10000 ten thousand	a'seret alafim	(ז) עֲשֶׂרֶת אֲלָפִים
one hundred thousand	'me'a 'elef	(ז) מֵאָה אֶלֶף
million	milyon	(ז) מִילְיוֹן
billion	milyard	(ז) מִילְיַארְד

3. Humans. Family

man (adult male)	'gever	(ז) גֶּבֶר
young man	baχur	(ז) בָּחוּר
teenager	'na'ar	(ז) נַעַר
woman	iʃa	(נ) אִשָּׁה
girl (young woman)	baχura	(נ) בַּחוּרָה
age	gil	(ז) גִּיל
adult (adj)	mevugar	(ז) מְבוּגָּר
middle-aged (adj)	bagil ha'amida	בַּגִּיל הָעֲמִידָה
elderly (adj)	zaken	זָקֵן
old (adj)	zaken	זָקֵן
old man	zaken	(ז) זָקֵן
old woman	zkena	(נ) זְקֵנָה
retirement	'pensya	(נ) פֶּנְסִיָה
to retire (from job)	latset legimla'ot	לָצֵאת לְגִימְלָאוֹת
retiree	pensyoner	(ז) פֶּנְסִיוֹנֶר

mother	em	אֵם (נ)
father	av	אָב (ז)
son	ben	בֵּן (ז)
daughter	bat	בַּת (נ)
brother	aχ	אָח (ז)
elder brother	aχ gadol	אָח גָדוֹל (ז)
younger brother	aχ katan	אָח קָטָן (ז)
sister	aχot	אָחוֹת (נ)
elder sister	aχot gdola	אָחוֹת גדוֹלָה (נ)
younger sister	aχot ktana	אָחוֹת קטָנָה (נ)
parents	horim	הוֹרִים (ז״ר)
child	'yeled	יֶלֶד (ז)
children	yeladim	יְלָדִים (ז״ר)
stepmother	em χoreget	אֵם חוֹרֶגֶת (נ)
stepfather	av χoreg	אָב חוֹרֵג (ז)
grandmother	'savta	סַבתָא (נ)
grandfather	'saba	סַבָּא (ז)
grandson	'neχed	נֶכֶד (ז)
granddaughter	neχda	נֶבדָה (נ)
grandchildren	neχadim	נְבָדִים (ז״ר)
uncle	dod	דוֹד (ז)
aunt	'doda	דוֹדָה (נ)
nephew	aχyan	אַחיָין (ז)
niece	aχyanit	אַחייָנִית (נ)
wife	iʃa	אִשָה (נ)
husband	'ba'al	בַּעַל (ז)
married (masc.)	nasui	נָשׂוּי
married (fem.)	nesu'a	נְשׂוּאָה
widow	almana	אַלמָנָה (נ)
widower	alman	אַלמָן (ז)
name (first name)	ʃem	שֵם (ז)
surname (last name)	ʃem miʃpaχa	שֵם מִשפָּחָה (ז)
relative	karov miʃpaχa	קָרוֹב מִשפָּחָה (ז)
friend (masc.)	χaver	חָבֵר (ז)
friendship	yedidut	יְדִידוּת (נ)
partner	ʃutaf	שוּתָף (ז)
superior (n)	memune	מְמוּנֶה (ז)
colleague	amit	עָמִית (ז)
neighbors	ʃχenim	שבֵנִים (ז״ר)

4. Human body

| organism (body) | guf ha'adam | גוּף הָאָדָם (ז) |
| body | guf | גוּף (ז) |

heart	lev	לֵב (ז)
blood	dam	דָם (ז)
brain	'moaχ	מוֹחַ (ז)
nerve	atsav	עָצָב (ז)

bone	'etsem	עֶצֶם (נ)
skeleton	'ʃeled	שֶׁלֶד (ז)
spine (backbone)	amud haʃidra	עַמוּד הַשִּׁדְרָה (ז)
rib	'tsela	צֵלָע (ז)
skull	gul'golet	גוּלגוֹלֶת (נ)

muscle	ʃrir	שְׁרִיר (ז)
lungs	re'ot	רֵיאוֹת (נ״ר)
skin	or	עוֹר (ז)

head	roʃ	ראש (ז)
face	panim	פָּנִים (ז״ר)
nose	af	אַף (ז)
forehead	'metsaχ	מֵצַח (ז)
cheek	'leχi	לֶחִי (נ)

mouth	pe	פֶּה (ז)
tongue	laʃon	לָשׁוֹן (נ)
tooth	ʃen	שֵׁן (נ)
lips	sfa'tayim	שְׂפָתַיִם (נ״ר)
chin	santer	סַנטֵר (ז)

ear	'ozen	אוֹזֶן (נ)
neck	tsavar	צַוָּאר (ז)
throat	garon	גָרוֹן (ז)

eye	'ayin	עַיִן (נ)
pupil	iʃon	אִישׁוֹן (ז)
eyebrow	gaba	גַבָּה (נ)
eyelash	ris	רִיס (ז)

hair	se'ar	שֵׂיעָר (ז)
hairstyle	tis'roket	תִסרוֹקֶת (נ)
mustache	safam	שָׂפָם (ז)
beard	zakan	זָקָן (ז)
to have (a beard, etc.)	legadel	לְגַדֵּל
bald (adj)	ke'reaχ	קֵירֵחַ

hand	kaf yad	כַּף יָד (נ)
arm	yad	יָד (נ)
finger	'etsba	אֶצבַּע (נ)
nail	tsi'poren	צִיפּוֹרֶן (ז)
palm	kaf yad	כַּף יָד (נ)

shoulder	katef	כָּתֵף (נ)
leg	'regel	רֶגֶל (נ)
foot	kaf 'regel	כַּף רֶגֶל (נ)

knee	'berex	בֶּרֶךְ (נ)
heel	akev	עָקֵב (ז)
back	gav	גַב (ז)
waist	'talya	טַלְיָה (נ)
beauty mark	nekudat xen	נְקוּדַת חֵן (נ)
birthmark (café au lait spot)	'ketem leida	כֶּתֶם לֵידָה (ז)

5. Medicine. Diseases. Drugs

health	bri'ut	בְּרִיאוּת (נ)
well (not sick)	bari	בָּרִיא
sickness	maxala	מַחֲלָה (נ)
to be sick	lihyot xole	לִהְיוֹת חוֹלֶה
ill, sick (adj)	xole	חוֹלֶה
cold (illness)	hitstanenut	הִצְטַנְנוּת (נ)
to catch a cold	lehitstanen	לְהִצְטַנֵן
tonsillitis	da'leket ʃkedim	דַלֶקֶת שְׁקֵדִים (נ)
pneumonia	da'leket re'ot	דַלֶקֶת רֵיאוֹת (נ)
flu, influenza	ʃa'pa'at	שַׁפַּעַת (נ)
runny nose (coryza)	na'zelet	נַזֶלֶת (נ)
cough	ʃi'ul	שִׁיעוּל (ז)
to cough (vi)	lehiʃta'el	לְהִשְׁתַעֵל
to sneeze (vi)	lehit'ateʃ	לְהִתְעַטֵשׁ
stroke	ʃavaʦ moxi	שָׁבָץ מוֹחִי (ז)
heart attack	hetkef lev	הֶתְקֵף לֵב (ז)
allergy	a'lergya	אָלֶרְגְיָה (נ)
asthma	'astma, ka'ʦeret	אַסְתְמָה, קַצֶרֶת (נ)
diabetes	su'keret	סוּכֶּרֶת (נ)
tumor	gidul	גִידוּל (ז)
cancer	sartan	סַרְטָן (ז)
alcoholism	alkoholizm	אַלְכּוֹהוֹלִיזְם (ז)
AIDS	eids	אֵיידְס (ז)
fever	ka'daxat	קַדַחַת (נ)
seasickness	maxalat yam	מַחֲלַת יָם (נ)
bruise (hématome)	xabura	חַבּוּרָה (נ)
bump (lump)	blita	בְּלִיטָה (נ)
to limp (vi)	liʦ'lo'a	לְצְלוֹעַ
dislocation	'neka	נֶקַע (ז)
to dislocate (vt)	lin'ko'a	לִנְקוֹעַ
fracture	'ʃever	שֶׁבֶר (ז)
burn (injury)	kviya	כְּוִויָה (נ)
injury	pʦi'a	פְּצִיעָה (נ)

| pain, ache | ke'ev | כְּאֵב (ז) |
| toothache | ke'ev ʃi'nayim | כְּאֵב שִׁינַיִים (ז) |

to sweat (perspire)	leha'zi'a	לְהַזִיעַ
deaf (adj)	xereʃ	חֵירֵשׁ
mute (adj)	ilem	אִילֵם

immunity	xasinut	חֲסִינוּת (נ)
virus	'virus	וִירוּס (ז)
microbe	xaidak	חַיְידָק (ז)
bacterium	bak'terya	בַּקְטֶרְיָה (נ)
infection	zihum	זִיהוּם (ז)

hospital	beit xolim	בֵּית חוֹלִים (ז)
cure	ripui	רִיפּוּי (ז)
to vaccinate (vt)	lexasen	לְחַסֵן
to be in a coma	lihyot betar'demet	לִהְיוֹת בְּתַרְדֶמֶת
intensive care	tipul nimraʦ	טִיפּוּל נִמְרָץ (ז)
symptom	simptom	סִימְפְּטוֹם (ז)
pulse	'dofek	דוֹפֶק (ז)

6. Feelings. Emotions. Conversation

I, me	ani	אֲנִי (ז, נ)
you (masc.)	ata	אַתָה (ז)
you (fem.)	at	אַתְ (נ)
he	hu	הוּא (ז)
she	hi	הִיא (נ)

we	a'naxnu	אֲנַחְנוּ (ז, נ)
you (masc.)	atem	אַתֶם (ז"ר)
you (fem.)	aten	אַתֶן (נ"ר)
you (polite, sing.)	ata, at	אַתָה (ז), אַתְ (נ)
you (polite, pl)	atem, aten	אַתֶם (ז"ר), אַתֶן (נ"ר)
they (masc.)	hem	הֵם (ז"ר)
they (fem.)	hen	הֵן (נ"ר)

Hello! (fam.)	ʃalom!	שָׁלוֹם!
Hello! (form.)	ʃalom!	שָׁלוֹם!
Good morning!	'boker tov!	בּוֹקֶר טוֹב!
Good afternoon!	ʦaha'rayim tovim!	צָהֳרַיִים טוֹבִים!
Good evening!	'erev tov!	עֶרֶב טוֹב!

to say hello	lomar ʃalom	לוֹמַר שָׁלוֹם
to greet (vt)	lomar ʃalom	לוֹמַר שָׁלוֹם
How are you? (form.)	ma ʃlomex?, ma ʃlomxa?	מַה שְׁלוֹמֵךְ? (נ), מַה שְׁלוֹמְךָ? (ז)
How are you? (fam.)	ma niʃma?	מַה נִשְׁמָע?
Bye-Bye! Goodbye!	lehitra'ot!	לְהִתְרָאוֹת!
Bye!	bai!	בַּיי!
Thank you!	toda!	תוֹדָה!

feelings	regaʃot	רְגָשׁוֹת (ז"ר)
to be hungry	lihyot ra'ev	לִהְיוֹת רָעֵב
to be thirsty	lihyot tsame	לִהְיוֹת צָמֵא
tired (adj)	ayef	עָיֵף
to be worried	lid'og	לִדְאוֹג
to be nervous	lihyot atsbani	לִהְיוֹת עַצְבָּנִי
hope	tikva	תִּקְוָה (נ)
to hope (vi, vt)	lekavot	לְקַוּוֹת
character	'ofi	אוֹפִי (ז)
modest (adj)	tsa'nu'a	צָנוּעַ
lazy (adj)	atsel	עָצֵל
generous (adj)	nadiv	נָדִיב
talented (adj)	muxʃar	מוּכְשָׁר
honest (adj)	yaʃar	יָשָׁר
serious (adj)	retsini	רְצִינִי
shy, timid (adj)	baiʃan	בַּיְישָׁן
sincere (adj)	ken	כֵּן
coward	paxdan	פַּחְדָן (ז)
to sleep (vi)	liʃon	לִישׁוֹן
dream	xalom	חֲלוֹם (ז)
bed	mita	מִיטָה (נ)
pillow	karit	כָּרִית (נ)
insomnia	nedudei ʃena	נְדוּדֵי שֵׁינָה (ז"ר)
to go to bed	la'lexet liʃon	לָלֶכֶת לִישׁוֹן
nightmare	siyut	סִיוּט (ז)
alarm clock	ʃa'on me'orer	שָׁעוֹן מְעוֹרֵר (ז)
smile	xiyux	חִיּוּךְ (ז)
to smile (vi)	lexayex	לְחַיֵּךְ
to laugh (vi)	litsxok	לִצְחוֹק
quarrel	riv	רִיב (ז)
insult	elbon	עֶלְבּוֹן (ז)
resentment	tina	טִינָה (נ)
angry (mad)	ka'us	כָּעוּס

7. Clothing. Personal accessories

clothes	bgadim	בְּגָדִים (ז"ר)
coat (overcoat)	me'il	מְעִיל (ז)
fur coat	me'il parva	מְעִיל פַּרְוָה (ז)
jacket (e.g., leather ~)	me'il katsar	מְעִיל קָצָר (ז)
raincoat (trenchcoat, etc.)	me'il 'geʃem	מְעִיל גֶּשֶׁם (ז)
shirt (button shirt)	xultsa	חוּלְצָה (נ)
pants	mixna'sayim	מִכְנָסַיִים (ז"ר)

suit jacket	ʒaket	זָ'קֶט (ז)
suit	xalifa	חֲלִיפָה (נ)
dress (frock)	simla	שִׂמְלָה (נ)
skirt	xatsa'it	חֲצָאִית (נ)
T-shirt	ti ʃert	טִי שֶׁרְט (ז)
bathrobe	xaluk raxatsa	חָלוּק רַחְצָה (ז)
pajamas	pi'dʒama	פִּיגָ'מָה (נ)
workwear	bigdei avoda	בִּגְדֵי עֲבוֹדָה (ז"ר)
underwear	levanim	לְבָנִים (ז"ר)
socks	gar'bayim	גַּרְבַּיִם (ז"ר)
bra	xaziya	חֲזִייָה (נ)
pantyhose	garbonim	גַּרְבּוֹנִים (ז"ר)
stockings (thigh highs)	garbei 'nailon	גַּרְבֵּי נַיְלוֹן (ז"ר)
bathing suit	'beged yam	בֶּגֶד יָם (ז)
hat	'kova	כּוֹבַע (ז)
footwear	han'ala	הַנְעָלָה (נ)
boots (e.g., cowboy ~)	maga'fayim	מַגָּפַיִם (ז"ר)
heel	akev	עָקֵב (ז)
shoestring	srox	שְׂרוֹךְ (ז)
shoe polish	miʃxat na'a'layim	מִשְׁחַת נַעֲלַיִם (נ)
cotton (n)	kutna	כּוּתְנָה (נ)
wool (n)	'tsemer	צֶמֶר (ז)
fur (n)	parva	פַּרְוָוה (נ)
gloves	kfafot	כְּפָפוֹת (נ"ר)
mittens	kfafot	כְּפָפוֹת (נ"ר)
scarf (muffler)	tsa'if	צָעִיף (ז)
glasses (eyeglasses)	miʃka'fayim	מִשְׁקָפַיִם (ז"ר)
umbrella	mitriya	מַטְרִייָה (נ)
tie (necktie)	aniva	עֲנִיבָה (נ)
handkerchief	mimxata	מִמְחָטָה (נ)
comb	masrek	מַסְרֵק (ז)
hairbrush	miv'reʃet se'ar	מִבְרֶשֶׁת שֵׂיעָר (נ)
buckle	avzam	אַבְזָם (ז)
belt	xagora	חֲגוֹרָה (נ)
purse	tik	תִּיק (ז)
collar	tsavaron	צַווָארוֹן (ז)
pocket	kis	כִּיס (ז)
sleeve	ʃarvul	שַׁרְווּל (ז)
fly (on trousers)	xanut	חֲנוּת (נ)
zipper (fastener)	roxsan	רוֹכְסָן (ז)
button	kaftor	כַּפְתּוֹר (ז)
to get dirty (vi)	lehitlaxlex	לְהִתְלַכְלֵךְ
stain (mark, spot)	'ketem	כֶּתֶם (ז)

8. City. Urban institutions

store	χanut	חֲנוּת (נ)
shopping mall	kanyon	קַנְיוֹן (ז)
supermarket	super'market	סוּפֶּרְמַרְקֶט (ז)
shoe store	χanut na'a'layim	חֲנוּת נַעֲלַיִים (נ)
bookstore	χanut sfarim	חֲנוּת סְפָרִים (נ)
drugstore, pharmacy	beit mir'kaχat	בֵּית מִרְקַחַת (ז)
bakery	ma'afiya	מַאֲפִיָּה (נ)
pastry shop	χanut mamtakim	חֲנוּת מַמְתַקִים (נ)
grocery store	ma'kolet	מַכּוֹלֶת (נ)
butcher shop	itliz	אִטְלִיז (ז)
produce store	χanut perot viyerakot	חֲנוּת פֵּירוֹת וְיָרָקוֹת (נ)
market	ʃuk	שׁוּק (ז)
hair salon	mispara	מִסְפָּרָה (נ)
post office	'do'ar	דוֹאַר (ז)
dry cleaners	nikui yaveʃ	נִיקוּי יָבֵשׁ (ז)
circus	kirkas	קִרְקָס (ז)
zoo	gan hayot	גַּן חַיוֹת (ז)
theater	te'atron	תֵיאַטרוֹן (ז)
movie theater	kol'no'a	קוֹלְנוֹעַ (ז)
museum	muze'on	מוּזֵיאוֹן (ז)
library	sifriya	סִפְרִיָּה (נ)
mosque	misgad	מִסְגָּד (ז)
synagogue	beit 'kneset	בֵּית כְּנֶסֶת (ז)
cathedral	kated'rala	קָתֶדְרָלָה (נ)
temple	mikdaʃ	מִקְדָשׁ (ז)
church	knesiya	כְּנֵסִיָּה (נ)
college	miχlala	מִכְלָלָה (נ)
university	uni'versita	אוּנִיבֶּרְסִיטָה (נ)
school	beit 'sefer	בֵּית סֵפֶר (ז)
hotel	beit malon	בֵּית מָלוֹן (ז)
bank	bank	בַּנק (ז)
embassy	ʃagrirut	שַׁגְרִירוּת (נ)
travel agency	soχnut nesi'ot	סוֹכְנוּת נְסִיעוֹת (נ)
subway	ra'kevet taχtit	רַכֶּבֶת תַחְתִּית (נ)
hospital	beit χolim	בֵּית חוֹלִים (ז)
gas station	taχanat 'delek	תַחֲנַת דֶלֶק (נ)
parking lot	migraʃ χanaya	מִגְרַשׁ חֲנָיָה (ז)
ENTRANCE	knisa	כְּנִיסָה
EXIT	yetsi'a	יְצִיאָה
PUSH	dχof	דחוֹף
PULL	mʃoχ	משוֹך

| OPEN | pa'tuax | פָּתוּחַ |
| CLOSED | sagur | סָגוּר |

monument	an'darta	אַנְדַּרְטָה (נ)
fortress	mivtsar	מִבְצָר (ז)
palace	armon	אַרְמוֹן (ז)

medieval (adj)	benaimi	בֵּינֵיימִי
ancient (adj)	atik	עָתִיק
national (adj)	le'umi	לְאוֹמִי
famous (monument, etc.)	mefursam	מְפוֹרְסָם

9. Money. Finances

money	'kesef	כֶּסֶף (ז)
coin	mat'be'a	מַטְבֵּעַ (ז)
dollar	'dolar	דוֹלָר (ז)
euro	'eiro	אֵירוֹ (ז)

ATM	kaspomat	כַּסְפּוֹמָט (ז)
currency exchange	misrad hamarat mat'be'a	מִשְׂרַד הֲמָרַת מַטְבֵּעַ (ז)
exchange rate	'ʃa'ar xalifin	שַׁעַר חֲלִיפִין (ז)
cash	mezuman	מְזוּמָן

How much?	'kama?	כַּמָּה?
to pay (vi, vt)	leʃalem	לְשַׁלֵּם
payment	taʃlum	תַּשְׁלוּם (ז)
change (give the ~)	'odef	עוֹדֶף (ז)

price	mexir	מְחִיר (ז)
discount	hanaxa	הֲנָחָה (נ)
cheap (adj)	zol	זוֹל
expensive (adj)	yakar	יָקָר

bank	bank	בַּנְק (ז)
account	xeʃbon	חֶשְׁבּוֹן (ז)
credit card	kartis aʃrai	כַּרְטִיס אַשְׁרַאי (ז)
check	tʃek	צֶ'ק (ז)
to write a check	lixtov tʃek	לִכְתּוֹב צֶ'ק
checkbook	pinkas 'tʃekim	פִּנְקַס צֶ'קִים (ז)

debt	xov	חוֹב (ז)
debtor	'ba'al xov	בַּעַל חוֹב (ז)
to lend (money)	lehalvot	לְהַלְווֹת
to borrow (vi, vt)	lilvot	לִלְווֹת

to rent (~ a tuxedo)	liskor	לִשְׂכֹּר
on credit (adv)	be'aʃrai	בְּאַשְׁרַאי
wallet	arnak	אַרְנָק (ז)
safe	ka'sefet	כַּסֶּפֶת (נ)

inheritance	yeruʃa	יְרוּשָׁה (נ)
fortune (wealth)	'oʃer	עוֹשֶׁר (ז)
tax	mas	מַס (ז)
fine	knas	קְנָס (ז)
to fine (vt)	liknos	לִקְנוֹס
wholesale (adj)	sitona'i	סִיטוֹנָאִי
retail (adj)	kim'oni	קִמְעוֹנִי
to insure (vt)	leva'teaχ	לְבַטֵּחַ
insurance	bi'tuaχ	בִּיטוּחַ (ז)
capital	hon	הוֹן (ז)
turnover	maχzor	מַחְזוֹר (ז)
stock (share)	menaya	מְנָיָה (נ)
profit	'revaχ	רֶווַח (ז)
profitable (adj)	rivχi	רְווּחִי
crisis	maʃber	מַשְׁבֵּר (ז)
bankruptcy	pʃitat 'regel	פְּשִׁיטַת רֶגֶל (נ)
to go bankrupt	liʃot 'regel	לִפְשׁוֹט רֶגֶל
accountant	ro'e χeʃbon	רוֹאֵה חֶשְׁבּוֹן (ז)
salary	mas'koret	מַשְׂכּוֹרֶת (נ)
bonus (money)	'bonus	בּוֹנוּס (ז)

10. Transportation

bus	'otobus	אוֹטוֹבּוּס (ז)
streetcar	ra'kevet kala	רַכֶּבֶת קַלָּה (נ)
trolley bus	tro'leibus	טְרוֹלֵיבּוּס (ז)
to go by …	lin'so'a be…	לִנְסוֹעַ בְּ...
to get on (~ the bus)	la'alot	לַעֲלוֹת
to get off …	la'redet mi…	לָרֶדֶת מִ...
stop (e.g., bus ~)	taχana	תַּחֲנָה (נ)
terminus	hataχana ha'aχrona	הַתַּחֲנָה הָאַחֲרוֹנָה (נ)
schedule	'luaχ zmanim	לוּחַ זְמַנִּים (ז)
ticket	kartis	כַּרְטִיס (ז)
to be late (for …)	le'aχer	לְאַחֵר
taxi, cab	monit	מוֹנִית (נ)
by taxi	bemonit	בְּמוֹנִית
taxi stand	taχanat moniyot	תַּחֲנַת מוֹנִיּוֹת (נ)
traffic	tnu'a	תְּנוּעָה (נ)
rush hour	ʃa'ot 'omes	שְׁעוֹת עוֹמֶס (נ-ר)
to park (vi)	laχanot	לַחֲנוֹת
subway	ra'kevet taχtit	רַכֶּבֶת תַּחְתִּית (נ)

station	taxana	תַחֲנָה (נ)
train	ra'kevet	רַכֶּבֶת (נ)
train station	taxanat ra'kevet	תַחֲנַת רַכֶּבֶת (נ)
rails	mesilot	מְסִילוֹת (נ"ר)
compartment	ta	תָא (ז)
berth	dargaʃ	דַרגָש (ז)
airplane	matos	מָטוֹס (ז)
air ticket	kartis tisa	כַּרטִיס טִיסָה (ז)
airline	xevrat te'ufa	חֶבְרַת תְעוּפָה (נ)
airport	nemal te'ufa	נְמַל תְעוּפָה (ז)
flight (act of flying)	tisa	טִיסָה (נ)
luggage	kvuda	כְּבוּדָה (נ)
luggage cart	eglat kvuda	עֶגלַת כְּבוּדָה (נ)
ship	sfina	סְפִינָה (נ)
cruise ship	oniyat ta'anugot	אוֹנִיַית תַעֲנוּגוֹת (נ)
yacht	'yaxta	יַכטָה (נ)
boat (flat-bottomed ~)	sira	סִירָה (נ)
captain	rav xovel	רַב־חוֹבֵל (ז)
cabin	ta	תָא (ז)
port (harbor)	namal	נָמָל (ז)
bicycle	ofa'nayim	אוֹפַנַיים (ז"ר)
scooter	kat'no'a	קַטנוֹעַ (ז)
motorcycle, bike	of'no'a	אוֹפנוֹעַ (ז)
pedal	davʃa	דַוושָה (נ)
pump	maʃeva	מַשאֵבָה (נ)
wheel	galgal	גַלגַל (ז)
automobile, car	mexonit	מְכוֹנִית (נ)
ambulance	'ambulans	אַמבּוּלַנס (ז)
truck	masa'it	מַשָׂאִית (נ)
used (adj)	meʃumaʃ	מְשוּמָש
car crash	te'una	תְאוּנָה (נ)
repair	ʃiputs	שִיפּוּץ (ז)

11. Food. Part 1

meat	basar	בָּשָׂר (ז)
chicken	of	עוֹף (ז)
duck	barvaz	בַּרוָז (ז)
pork	basar xazir	בְּשַׂר חֲזִיר (ז)
veal	basar 'egel	בְּשַׂר עֵגֶל (ז)
lamb	basar 'keves	בְּשַׂר כֶּבֶש (ז)
beef	bakar	בָּקָר (ז)
sausage (bologna, pepperoni, etc.)	naknik	נַקנִיק (ז)

egg	beitsa	בֵּיצָה (נ)
fish	dag	דָּג (ז)
cheese	gvina	גבִינָה (נ)
sugar	sukar	סוּכָּר (ז)
salt	'melax	מֶלַח (ז)
rice	'orez	אוֹרֶז (ז)
pasta (macaroni)	'pasta	פַּסטָה (נ)
butter	xem'a	חֶמאָה (נ)
vegetable oil ·	'ʃemen tsimxi	שֶׁמֶן צָמחִי (ז)
bread	'lexem	לֶחֶם (ז)
chocolate (n)	'ʃokolad	שׁוֹקוֹלָד (ז)
wine	'yayin	יַיִן (ז)
coffee	kafe	קָפֶּה (ז)
milk	xalav	חָלָב (ז)
juice	mits	מִיץ (ז)
beer	'bira	בִּירָה (נ)
tea	te	תֵּה (ז)
tomato	agvaniya	עַגבָנִייָה (נ)
cucumber	melafefon	מְלָפְפוֹן (ז)
carrot	'gezer	גֶּזֶר (ז)
potato	ta'puax adama	תַּפּוּחַ אֲדָמָה (ז)
onion	batsal	בָּצָל (ז)
garlic	ʃum	שׁוּם (ז)
cabbage	kruv	כּרוּב (ז)
beetroot	'selek	סֶלֶק (ז)
eggplant	xatsil	חָצִיל (ז)
dill	ʃamir	שָׁמִיר (ז)
lettuce	'xasa	חַסָּה (נ)
corn (maize)	'tiras	תִּירָס (ז)
fruit	pri	פּרִי (ז)
apple	ta'puax	תַּפּוּחַ (ז)
pear	agas	אַגָּס (ז)
lemon	limon	לִימוֹן (ז)
orange	tapuz	תַּפּוּז (ז)
strawberry (garden ~)	tut sade	תּוּת שָׂדֶה (ז)
plum	ʃezif	שׁזִיף (ז)
raspberry	'petel	פֶּטֶל (ז)
pineapple	'ananas	אֲנָנָס (ז)
banana	ba'nana	בַּנָנָה (נ)
watermelon	ava'tiax	אֲבַטִיחַ (ז)
grape	anavim	עֲנָבִים (ז"ר)
melon	melon	מָלוֹן (ז)

12. Food. Part 2

cuisine	mitbaχ	מִטְבָּח (ז)
recipe	matkon	מַתְכּוֹן (ז)
food	'oχel	אוֹכָל (ז)
to have breakfast	le'eχol aruχat 'boker	לֶאֱכוֹל אֲרוּחַת בּוֹקֶר
to have lunch	le'eχol aruχat tsaha'rayim	לֶאֱכוֹל אֲרוּחַת צָהֳרַיִים
to have dinner	le'eχol aruχat 'erev	לֶאֱכוֹל אֲרוּחַת עֶרֶב
taste, flavor	'ta'am	טַעַם (ז)
tasty (adj)	ta'im	טָעִים
cold (adj)	kar	קַר
hot (adj)	χam	חַם
sweet (sugary)	matok	מָתוֹק
salty (adj)	ma'luaχ	מָלוּחַ
sandwich (bread)	kariχ	כָּרִיךְ (ז)
side dish	to'sefet	תּוֹסֶפֶת (נ)
filling (for cake, pie)	milui	מִילוּי (ז)
sauce	'rotev	רוֹטֶב (ז)
piece (of cake, pie)	χatiχa	חֲתִיכָה (נ)
diet	di''eta	דִּיאֶטָה (נ)
vitamin	vitamin	וִיטָמִין (ז)
calorie	ka'lorya	קָלוֹרִיָה (נ)
vegetarian (n)	tsimχoni	צִמְחוֹנִי (ז)
restaurant	mis'ada	מִסְעָדָה (נ)
coffee house	beit kafe	בֵּית קָפֶה (ז)
appetite	te'avon	תֵּיאָבוֹן (ז)
Enjoy your meal!	betei'avon!	בְּתֵיאָבוֹן!
waiter	meltsar	מֶלְצָר (ז)
waitress	meltsarit	מֶלְצָרִית (נ)
bartender	'barmen	בַּרְמֶן (ז)
menu	tafrit	תַּפְרִיט (ז)
spoon	kaf	כַּף (נ)
knife	sakin	סַכִּין (ז, נ)
fork	mazleg	מַזְלֵג (ז)
cup (e.g., coffee ~)	'sefel	סֵפֶל (ז)
plate (dinner ~)	tsa'laχat	צַלַחַת (נ)
saucer	taχtit	תַּחְתִּית (נ)
napkin (on table)	mapit	מַפִּית (נ)
toothpick	keisam ʃi'nayim	קִיסָם שִׁינַיִים (ז)
to order (meal)	lehazmin	לְהַזְמִין
course, dish	mana	מָנָה (נ)
portion	mana	מָנָה (נ)

appetizer	meta'aven	מְתַאֲבֵן (ז)
salad	salat	סָלָט (ז)
soup	marak	מָרָק (ז)
dessert	ki'nuax	קִינוּחַ (ז)
jam (whole fruit jam)	riba	רִיבָּה (נ)
ice-cream	'glida	גלִידָה (נ)
check	xeʃbon	חֶשׁבּוֹן (ז)
to pay the check	leʃalem	לְשַׁלֵם
tip	tip	טִיפ (ז)

13. House. Apartment. Part 1

house	'bayit	בַּיִת (ז)
country house	'bayit bakfar	בַּיִת בַּכּפָר (ז)
villa (seaside ~)	'vila	וִילָה (נ)
floor, story	'koma	קוֹמָה (נ)
entrance	knisa	כּנִיסָה (נ)
wall	kir	קִיר (ז)
roof	gag	גג (ז)
chimney	aruba	אֲרוּבָּה (נ)
attic (storage place)	aliyat gag	עֲלִיַת גג (נ)
window	xalon	חַלוֹן (ז)
window ledge	'eden xalon	אֶדֶן חַלוֹן (ז)
balcony	mir'peset	מִרפֶּסֶת (נ)
stairs (stairway)	madregot	מַדרֵגוֹת (נ"ר)
mailbox	teivat 'do'ar	תֵּיבַת דוֹאַר (נ)
garbage can	pax 'zevel	פַּח זֶבֶל (ז)
elevator	ma'alit	מַעֲלִית (נ)
electricity	xaʃmal	חַשׁמַל (ז)
light bulb	nura	נוּרָה (נ)
switch	'meteg	מֶתֶג (ז)
wall socket	'ʃeka	שֶׁקַע (ז)
fuse	natix	נָתִיך (ז)
door	'delet	דֶלֶת (נ)
handle, doorknob	yadit	יָדִית (נ)
key	maf'teax	מַפתֵחַ (ז)
doormat	ʃtixon	שׁטִיחוֹן (ז)
door lock	man'ul	מַנעוּל (ז)
doorbell	pa'amon	פַּעֲמוֹן (ז)
knock (at the door)	hakaʃa	הַקָשָׁה (נ)
to knock (vi)	lehakiʃ	לְהַקִישׁ
peephole	einit	עֵינִית (נ)
yard	xatser	חָצֵר (נ)

garden	gan	גַּן (ז)
swimming pool	breχat sχiya	בְּרִיכַת שׂחִיָיה (נ)
gym (home gym)	'χeder 'koʃer	חֶדָר כּוֹשֶׁר (ז)
tennis court	migraʃ 'tenis	מִגרַשׁ טֶנִיס (ז)
garage	musaχ	מוּסָךְ (ז)

private property	reχuʃ prati	רְכוּשׁ פְּרָטִי (ז)
warning sign	'ʃelet azhara	שֶׁלֶט אַזהָרָה (ז)
security	avtaχa	אַבטָחָה (נ)
security guard	ʃomer	שׁוֹמֵר (ז)

renovations	ʃiputs	שִׁיפּוּץ (ז)
to renovate (vt)	leʃapets	לְשַׁפֵּץ
to put in order	lesader	לְסַדֵּר
to paint (~ a wall)	lits'bo'a	לִצבּוֹעַ
wallpaper	tapet	טַפֶּט (ז)
to varnish (vt)	lim'roaχ 'laka	לִמרוֹחַ לַכָּה

pipe	tsinor	צִינוֹר (ז)
tools	klei avoda	כְּלֵי עֲבוֹדָה (ז"ר)
basement	martef	מַרתֵף (ז)
sewerage (system)	biyuv	בִּיוּב (ז)

14. House. Apartment. Part 2

apartment	dira	דִירָה (נ)
room	'χeder	חֶדֶר (ז)
bedroom	χadar ʃena	חֲדַר שֵׁינָה (ז)
dining room	pinat 'oχel	פִּינַת אוֹכֶל (נ)

living room	salon	סָלוֹן (ז)
study (home office)	χadar avoda	חֲדַר עֲבוֹדָה (ז)
entry room	prozdor	פּרוֹזדוֹר (ז)
bathroom (room with a bath or shower)	χadar am'batya	חֲדַר אַמבַּטיָה (ז)
half bath	ʃerutim	שֵׁירוּתִים (ז"ר)

| floor | ritspa | רִצפָּה (נ) |
| ceiling | tikra | תִקרָה (נ) |

to dust (vt)	lenakot avak	לְנַקוֹת אָבָק
vacuum cleaner	ʃo'ev avak	שׁוֹאֵב אָבָק (ז)
to vacuum (vt)	liʃov avak	לִשׁאוֹב אָבָק

mop	magev im smartut	מַגֵב עִם סמַרטוּט (ז)
dust cloth	smartut avak	סמַרטוּט אָבָק (ז)
short broom	mat'ate katan	מַטאָטֵא קָטָן (ז)
dustpan	ya'e	יָעֶה (ז)
furniture	rehitim	רָהִיטִים (ז"ר)
table	ʃulχan	שׁוּלחָן (ז)

chair	kise	כָּסֵא (ז)
armchair	kursa	כּוּרסָה (נ)
bookcase	aron sfarim	אֲרוֹן סְפָרִים (ז)
shelf	madaf	מַדָף (ז)
wardrobe	aron bgadim	אֲרוֹן בְּגָדִים (ז)
mirror	mar'a	מַרְאָה (נ)
carpet	ʃa'tiaχ	שָׁטִיחַ (ז)
fireplace	aχ	אָח (נ)
drapes	vilonot	וִילוֹנוֹת (ז"ר)
table lamp	menorat ʃulχan	מְנוֹרַת שׁוּלחָן (נ)
chandelier	niv'reʃet	נִברֶשֶׁת (נ)
kitchen	mitbaχ	מִטבָּח (ז)
gas stove (range)	tanur gaz	תַנוּר גָז (ז)
electric stove	tanur χaʃmali	תַנוּר חַשְׁמַלִי (ז)
microwave oven	mikrogal	מִיקרוֹגַל (ז)
refrigerator	mekarer	מְקָרֵר (ז)
freezer	makpi	מַקפִּיא (ז)
dishwasher	me'diaχ kelim	מֵדִיחַ כֵּלִים (ז)
faucet	'berez	בֶּרֶז (ז)
meat grinder	matχenat basar	מַטחֵנַת בָּשָׂר (נ)
juicer	masχeta	מַסחֵטָה (נ)
toaster	'toster	טוֹסטֶר (ז)
mixer	'mikser	מִיקסֶר (ז)
coffee machine	meχonat kafe	מְכוֹנַת קָפֶה (נ)
kettle	kumkum	קוּמקוּם (ז)
teapot	kumkum	קוּמקוּם (ז)
TV set	tele'vizya	טֶלֶוִוזִיָה (נ)
VCR (video recorder)	maχʃir 'vide'o	מַכשִׁיר וִידֵאוֹ (ז)
iron (e.g., steam ~)	magheʦ	מַגהֵץ (ז)
telephone	'telefon	טֶלֶפוֹן (ז)

15. Professions. Social status

director	menahel	מְנַהֵל (ז)
superior	memune	מְמוּנֶה (ז)
president	nasi	נָשִׂיא (ז)
assistant	ozer	עוֹזֵר (ז)
secretary	mazkir	מַזכִּיר (ז)
owner, proprietor	be'alim	בְּעָלִים (ז)
partner	ʃutaf	שׁוּתָף (ז)
stockholder	'ba'al menayot	בַּעַל מְנָיוֹת (ז)
businessman	iʃ asakim	אִיש עֲסָקִים (ז)

millionaire	milyoner	מִילְיוֹנֶר (ז)
billionaire	milyarder	מִילְיַארְדֶר (ז)
actor	saχkan	שַׂחְקָן (ז)
architect	adriχal	אַדְרִיכָל (ז)
banker	bankai	בַּנְקַאי (ז)
broker	soχen	סוֹכֵן (ז)
veterinarian	veterinar	וֶטֶרִינָר (ז)
doctor	rofe	רוֹפֵא (ז)
chambermaid	χadranit	חַדְרָנִית (נ)
designer	me'atsev	מְעַצֵב (ז)
correspondent	katav	כַּתָב (ז)
delivery man	ʃa'liaχ	שָׁלִיח (ז)
electrician	χaʃmalai	חַשְׁמַלַאי (ז)
musician	muzikai	מוּזִיקַאי (ז)
babysitter	ʃmartaf	שמַרטָף (ז)
hairdresser	sapar	סַפָּר (ז)
herder, shepherd	ro'e tson	רוֹעֵה צֹאן (ז)
singer (masc.)	zamar	זַמָר (ז)
translator	metargem	מְתַרְגֵם (ז)
writer	sofer	סוֹפֵר (ז)
carpenter	nagar	נַגָר (ז)
cook	tabaχ	טַבָּח (ז)
fireman	kabai	כַּבַּאי (ז)
police officer	ʃoter	שׁוֹטֵר (ז)
mailman	davar	דַוָר (ז)
programmer	metaχnet	מְתַכְנֵת (ז)
salesman (store staff)	moχer	מוֹכֵר (ז)
worker	po'el	פּוֹעֵל (ז)
gardener	ganan	גַנָן (ז)
plumber	ʃravrav	שׁרַבְרָב (ז)
dentist	rofe ʃi'nayim	רוֹפֵא שִׁנַיִים (ז)
flight attendant (fem.)	da'yelet	דַיֶלֶת (נ)
dancer (masc.)	rakdan	רַקְדָן (ז)
bodyguard	ʃomer roʃ	שׁוֹמֵר רֹאשׁ (ז)
scientist	mad'an	מַדְעָן (ז)
schoolteacher	more	מוֹרֶה (ז)
farmer	χavai	חַוַואי (ז)
surgeon	kirurg	כִּירוּרג (ז)
miner	kore	כּוֹרֶה (ז)
chef (kitchen chef)	ʃef	שֶׁף (ז)
driver	nahag	נַהָג (ז)

16. Sport

kind of sports	anaf sport	עֶנַף סְפּוֹרט (ז)
soccer	kadu'regel	כַּדוּרֶגֶל (ז)
hockey	'hoki	הוֹקִי (ז)
basketball	kadursal	כַּדוּרסַל (ז)
baseball	'beisbol	בֵּייסבּוֹל (ז)
volleyball	kadur'af	כַּדוּרעָף (ז)
boxing	igruf	אִיגרוּף (ז)
wrestling	he'avkut	הֵיאָבקוּת (נ)
tennis	'tenis	טֶנִיס (ז)
swimming	sҳiya	שֹׂחִייָה (נ)
chess	'ʃaҳmat	שַׁחמָט (ז)
running	ritsa	רִיצָה (נ)
athletics	at'letika kala	אַתלֶטִיקָה קַלָה (נ)
figure skating	haҳlaka omanutit	הַחלָקָה אוֹמָנוּתִית (נ)
cycling	reҳiva al ofa'nayim	רְכִיבָה עַל אוֹפַנַּיִים (נ)
billiards	bilyard	בִּיליַארד (ז)
bodybuilding	pi'tuaҳ guf	פִּיתוּחַ גוּף (ז)
golf	golf	גוֹלף (ז)
scuba diving	tslila	צלִילָה (נ)
sailing	'ʃayit	שַׁיִט (ז)
archery	kaʃatut	קַשָׁתוּת (נ)
period, half	maҳatsit	מַחֲצִית (נ)
half-time	hafsaka	הַפסָקָה (נ)
tie	'teku	תֵּיקוּ (ז)
to tie (vi)	lesayem be'teku	לְסַיֵים בְּתֵיקוּ
treadmill	haliҳon	הֲלִיכוֹן (ז)
player	saҳkan	שַׂחקָן (ז)
substitute	saҳkan maҳlif	שַׂחקָן מַחלִיף (ז)
substitutes bench	safsal maҳlifim	סַפסַל מַחלִיפִים (ז)
match	misҳak	מִשֹׂחָק (ז)
goal	'ʃa'ar	שַׁעַר (ז)
goalkeeper	ʃo'er	שׁוֹעֵר (ז)
goal (score)	'ʃa'ar	שַׁעַר (ז)
Olympic Games	hamisҳakim ha'o'limpiyim	הַמִשֹׂחָקִים הָאוֹלִימפִּיִים (ז״ר)
to set a record	lik'bo'a si	לִקבּוֹעַ שִׂיא
final	gmar	גמָר (ז)
champion	aluf	אַלוּף (ז)
championship	alifut	אַלִיפוּת (נ)
winner	mena'tseaҳ	מְנַצֵחַ (ז)
victory	nitsaҳon	נִיצָחוֹן (ז)
to win (vi)	lena'tseaҳ	לְנַצֵחַ

to lose (not win)	lehafsid	לְהַפְסִיד
medal	me'dalya	מֶדַלְיָה (נ)
first place	makom riʃon	מָקוֹם רִאשׁוֹן (ז)
second place	makom ʃeni	מָקוֹם שֵׁנִי (ז)
third place	makom ʃliʃi	מָקוֹם שְׁלִישִׁי (ז)
stadium	itstadyon	אִצְטַדְיוֹן (ז)
fan, supporter	ohed	אוֹהֵד (ז)
trainer, coach	me'amen	מְאַמֵן (ז)
training	imun	אִימוּן (ז)

17. Foreign languages. Orthography

language	safa	שָׂפָה (נ)
to study (M)	lilmod	לִלְמוֹד
pronunciation	hagiya	הֲגִיָה (נ)
accent	mivta	מִבְטָא (ז)
noun	ʃem 'etsem	שֵׁם עֶצֶם (ז)
adjective	ʃem 'to'ar	שֵׁם תוֹאַר (ז)
verb	po'el	פּוֹעַל (ז)
adverb	'to'ar 'po'al	תוֹאַר פּוֹעַל (ז)
pronoun	ʃem guf	שֵׁם גוּף (ז)
interjection	milat kri'a	מִילַת קְרִיאָה (נ)
preposition	milat 'yaχas	מִילַת יַחַס (נ)
root	'ʃoreʃ	שׁוֹרֶשׁ (ז)
ending	si'yomet	סִיוֹמֶת (נ)
prefix	tχilit	תְחִילִית (נ)
syllable	havara	הֲבָרָה (נ)
suffix	si'yomet	סִיוֹמֶת (נ)
stress mark	'ta'am	טַעַם (ז)
period, dot	nekuda	נְקוּדָה (נ)
comma	psik	פְּסִיק (ז)
colon	nekudo'tayim	נְקוּדוֹתַיִים (נ״ר)
ellipsis	ʃaloʃ nekudot	שָׁלוֹשׁ נְקוּדוֹת (נ״ר)
question	ʃe'ela	שְׁאֵלָה (נ)
question mark	siman ʃe'ela	סִימַן שְׁאֵלָה (ז)
exclamation point	siman kri'a	סִימַן קְרִיאָה (ז)
in quotation marks	bemerχa'ot	בְּמֵרְכָאוֹת
in parenthesis	besog'rayim	בְּסוֹגְרַיִים
letter	ot	אוֹת (נ)
capital letter	ot gdola	אוֹת גְדוֹלָה (נ)
sentence	miʃpat	מִשְׁפָּט (ז)
group of words	tsiruf milim	צֵירוּף מִילִים (ז)

expression	bitui	בִּיטוּי (ז)
subject	nose	נוֹשֵׂא (ז)
predicate	nasu	נָשׂוּא (ז)
line	ʃura	שׁוּרָה (נ)
paragraph	piska	פִּסְקָה (נ)
synonym	mila nir'defet	מִילָה נִרְדֶפֶת (נ)
antonym	'hefeχ	הֶפֶךְ (ז)
exception	yotse min haklal	יוֹצֵא מִן הַכְּלָל (ז)
to underline (vt)	lehadgiʃ	לְהַדְגִיש
rules	klalim	כְּלָלִים (ז״ר)
grammar	dikduk	דִקְדוּק (ז)
vocabulary	otsar milim	אוֹצַר מִילִים (ז)
phonetics	torat ha'hege	תוֹרַת הַהֶגֶה (נ)
alphabet	alefbeit	אָלֶפְבֵּית (ז)
textbook	'sefer limud	סֵפֶר לִימוּד (ז)
dictionary	milon	מִילוֹן (ז)
phrasebook	siχon	שִׂיחוֹן (ז)
word	mila	מִילָה (נ)
meaning	maʃma'ut	מַשְׁמָעוּת (נ)
memory	zikaron	זִיכָּרוֹן (ז)

18. The Earth. Geography

the Earth	kadur ha''arets	כַּדוּר הָאָרֶץ (ז)
the globe (the Earth)	kadur ha''arets	כַּדוּר הָאָרֶץ (ז)
planet	koχav 'leχet	כּוֹכַב לֶכֶת (ז)
geography	ge'o'grafya	גֵיאוֹגְרַפְיָה (נ)
nature	'teva	טֶבַע (ז)
map	mapa	מַפָּה (נ)
atlas	'atlas	אַטְלָס (ז)
in the north	batsafon	בַּצָפוֹן
in the south	badarom	בַּדָרוֹם
in the west	bama'arav	בַּמַעֲרָב
in the east	bamizraχ	בַּמִזְרָח
sea	yam	יָם (ז)
ocean	ok'yanos	אוֹקְיָאנוֹס (ז)
gulf (bay)	mifrats	מִפְרָץ (ז)
straits	meitsar	מֵיצַר (ז)
continent (mainland)	ya'beʃet	יַבֶּשֶׁת (נ)
island	i	אִי (ז)
peninsula	χatsi i	חֲצִי אִי (ז)
archipelago	arχipelag	אַרְכִיפֶּלָג (ז)

harbor	namal	נָמָל (ז)
coral reef	ʃunit almogim	שׁוּנִית אַלְמוֹגִים (נ)
shore	χof	חוֹף (ז)
coast	χof yam	חוֹף יָם (ז)

| flow (flood tide) | ge'ut | גֵּאוּת (נ) |
| ebb (ebb tide) | 'ʃefel | שֵׁפֶל (ז) |

latitude	kav 'roχav	קו רוֹחַב (ז)
longitude	kav 'oreχ	קו אוֹרֶךְ (ז)
parallel	kav 'roχav	קו רוֹחַב (ז)
equator	kav hamaʃve	קו הַמַּשְׁוֶה (ז)

sky	ʃa'mayim	שָׁמַיִם (ז״ר)
horizon	'ofek	אוֹפֶק (ז)
atmosphere	atmos'fera	אַטמוֹספֵרָה (נ)

mountain	har	הַר (ז)
summit, top	pisga	פִּסגָּה (נ)
cliff	tsuk	צוּק (ז)
hill	giv'a	גִּבעָה (נ)

volcano	har 'ga'aʃ	הַר גַּעַשׁ (ז)
glacier	karχon	קַרחוֹן (ז)
waterfall	mapal 'mayim	מַפַּל מַיִם (ז)
plain	miʃor	מִישׁוֹר (ז)

river	nahar	נָהָר (ז)
spring (natural source)	ma'ayan	מַעיָן (ז)
bank (of river)	χof	חוֹף (ז)
downstream (adv)	bemorad hanahar	בְּמוֹרַד הַנָּהָר
upstream (adv)	bema'ale hanahar	בְּמַעֲלֵה הַנָּהָר

lake	agam	אֲגַם (ז)
dam	'seχer	סֶכֶר (ז)
canal	te'ala	תְּעָלָה (נ)
swamp (marshland)	bitsa	בִּיצָה (נ)
ice	'keraχ	קֶרַח (ז)

19. Countries of the world. Part 1

Europe	ei'ropa	אֵירוֹפָּה (נ)
European Union	ha'iχud ha'eiro'pe'i	הָאִיחוּד הָאֵירוֹפִּי (ז)
European (n)	eiro'pe'i	אֵירוֹפָּאִי (ז)
European (adj)	eiro'pe'i	אֵירוֹפָּאִי

Austria	'ostriya	אוֹסטרִיָה (נ)
Great Britain	bri'tanya hagdola	בּרִיטַניָה הַגדוֹלָה (נ)
England	'angliya	אַנגלִיָה (נ)
Belgium	'belgya	בֶּלגִיָה (נ)

Germany	ger'manya	גֶּרְמַנְיָה (נ)
Netherlands	'holand	הוֹלַנד (נ)
Holland	'holand	הוֹלַנד (נ)
Greece	yavan	יָוָון (נ)
Denmark	'denemark	דֶּנֶמַרְק (נ)
Ireland	'irland	אִירְלַנד (נ)

Iceland	'island	אִיסְלַנד (נ)
Spain	sfarad	סְפָרַד (נ)
Italy	i'talya	אִיטַלְיָה (נ)
Cyprus	kafrisin	קַפְרִיסִין (נ)
Malta	'malta	מַלְטָה (נ)

Norway	nor'vegya	נוֹרְבֶגְיָה (נ)
Portugal	portugal	פּוֹרְטוּגָל (נ)
Finland	'finland	פִינְלַנד (נ)
France	tsarfat	צָרְפַת (נ)
Sweden	'ʃvedya	שְבֶדְיָה (נ)

Switzerland	'ʃvaits	שְוַויץ (נ)
Scotland	'skotland	סְקוֹטְלַנד (נ)
Vatican	vatikan	וָתִיקָן (ז)
Liechtenstein	liχtenʃtain	לִיכְטֶנְשְטַיין (נ)
Luxembourg	luksemburg	לוקְסֶמְבּוֹרג (נ)

Monaco	mo'nako	מוֹנָקוֹ (נ)
Albania	al'banya	אַלְבַּנְיָה (נ)
Bulgaria	bul'garya	בּוּלְגַרְיָה (נ)

| Hungary | hun'garya | הוּנְגַרְיָה (נ) |
| Latvia | 'latviya | לַטְבְיָה (נ) |

Lithuania	'lita	לִיטָא (נ)
Poland	polin	פּוֹלִין (נ)
Romania	ro'manya	רוֹמַנְיָה (נ)

| Serbia | 'serbya | סֶרְבְיָה (נ) |
| Slovakia | slo'vakya | סְלוֹבַקְיָה (נ) |

Croatia	kro''atya	קְרוֹאַטְיָה (נ)
Czech Republic	'tʃeχya	צֶ'כְיָה (נ)
Estonia	es'tonya	אֶסְטוֹנְיָה (נ)

| Bosnia and Herzegovina | 'bosniya | בּוֹסְנְיָה (נ) |
| Macedonia (Republic of ~) | make'donya | מָקֶדוֹנְיָה (נ) |

Slovenia	slo'venya	סְלוֹבֶנְיָה (נ)
Montenegro	monte'negro	מוֹנְטֶנֶגְרוֹ (נ)
Belarus	'belarus	בֶּלָרוּס (נ)
Moldova, Moldavia	mol'davya	מוֹלְדַבְיָה (נ)
Russia	'rusya	רוּסְיָה (נ)
Ukraine	uk'rayna	אוּקְרַאִינָה (נ)

20. Countries of the world. Part 2

Asia	'asya	אַסְיָה (נ)
Vietnam	vyetnam	וְיֶטְנָאם (נ)
India	'hodu	הוֹדוּ (נ)
Israel	yisra'el	יִשְׂרָאֵל (נ)
China	sin	סִין (נ)

Lebanon	levanon	לְבָנוֹן (נ)
Mongolia	mon'golya	מוֹנגוֹלְיָה (נ)
Malaysia	ma'lezya	מָלֶזְיָה (נ)
Pakistan	pakistan	פָּקִיסטָן (נ)
Saudi Arabia	arav hasa'udit	עֲרָב הַסָעוּדִית (נ)

Thailand	'tailand	תַאילָנד (נ)
Taiwan	taivan	טַייוָון (נ)
Turkey	'turkiya	טוּרקִיָה (נ)
Japan	yapan	יָפָן (נ)
Afghanistan	afganistan	אַפגָנִיסטָן (נ)

Bangladesh	bangladeʃ	בַּנגלָדֶש (נ)
Indonesia	indo'nezya	אִינדוֹנֶזיָה (נ)
Jordan	yarden	יַרדֵן (נ)
Iraq	irak	עִירָאק (נ)
Iran	iran	אִירָן (נ)

Cambodia	kam'bodya	קַמבּוֹדיָה (נ)
Kuwait	kuveit	כּוּוֵית (נ)
Laos	la'os	לָאוֹס (נ)
Myanmar	miyanmar	מְיַאנמָר (נ)
Nepal	nepal	נֶפָּאל (נ)

United Arab Emirates	iχud ha'emi'royot ha'araviyot	אִיחוּד הָאֲמִירוֹיוֹת הָעֲרָבִיוֹת (ז)
Syria	'surya	סוּרִיָה (נ)
Palestine	falastin	פָּלֶסטִין (נ)
South Korea	ko'rei'a hadromit	קוֹרֵיאָה הַדרוֹמִית (נ)
North Korea	ko'rei'a hatsfonit	קוֹרֵיאָה הַצפוֹנִית (נ)

United States of America	artsot habrit	אַרצוֹת הַבּרִית (נ"ר)
Canada	'kanada	קָנָדָה (נ)
Mexico	'meksiko	מֶקסִיקוֹ (נ)
Argentina	argen'tina	אַרגֶנטִינָה (נ)
Brazil	brazil	בּרָזִיל (נ)

Colombia	ko'lombya	קוֹלוֹמבִּיָה (נ)
Cuba	'kuba	קוּבָּה (נ)
Chile	'tʃile	צִ'ילָה (נ)
Venezuela	venetsu''ela	וֶנֶצוּאֶלָה (נ)
Ecuador	ekvador	אֶקוָוֹדוֹר (נ)
The Bahamas	iyey ba'hama	אִיֵי בָּהָאמָה (ז"ר)

Panama	pa'nama	פָּנָמָה (נ)
Egypt	mits'rayim	מִצְרַיִם (נ)
Morocco	ma'roko	מָרוֹקוֹ (נ)
Tunisia	tu'nisya	טוּנִיסְיָה (נ)

Kenya	'kenya	קֶנְיָה (נ)
Libya	luv	לוּב (נ)
South Africa	drom 'afrika	דְּרוֹם אַפְרִיקָה (נ)
Australia	ost'ralya	אוֹסְטְרַלְיָה (נ)
New Zealand	nyu 'ziland	נִיוּ זִילַנְד (נ)

21. Weather. Natural disasters

weather	'mezeg avir	מֶזֶג אֲוִיר (ז)
weather forecast	taχazit 'mezeg ha'avir	תַּחֲזִית מֶזֶג הָאֲוִיר (נ)
temperature	tempera'tura	טֶמְפֶּרָטוּרָה (נ)
thermometer	madχom	מַדְחוֹם (ז)
barometer	ba'rometer	בָּרוֹמֶטֶר (ז)

sun	'femef	שֶׁמֶשׁ (נ)
to shine (vi)	lizhor	לִזְהוֹר
sunny (day)	fimfi	שִׁמְשִׁי
to come up (vi)	liz'roaχ	לִזְרוֹחַ
to set (vi)	lif'ko'a	לִשְׁקוֹעַ

rain	'gefem	גֶּשֶׁם (ז)
it's raining	yored 'gefem	יוֹרֵד גֶּשֶׁם
pouring rain	matar	מָטָר (ז)
rain cloud	av	עָב (ז)
puddle	fulit	שְׁלוּלִית (נ)
to get wet (in rain)	lehitratev	לְהִתְרַטֵּב

thunderstorm	sufat re'amim	סוּפַת רְעָמִים (נ)
lightning (~ strike)	barak	בָּרָק (ז)
to flash (vi)	livhok	לִבְהוֹק
thunder	'ra'am	רַעַם (ז)
it's thundering	lir'om	לִרְעוֹם
hail	barad	בָּרָד (ז)
it's hailing	yored barad	יוֹרֵד בָּרָד

heat (extreme ~)	χom	חוֹם (ז)
it's hot	χam	חַם
it's warm	χamim	חָמִים
it's cold	kar	קַר

fog (mist)	arapel	עֲרָפֶּל (ז)
foggy	me'urpal	מְעוּרְפָּל
cloud	anan	עָנָן (ז)
cloudy (adj)	me'unan	מְעוּנָן
humidity	laχut	לַחוּת (נ)

snow	'ʃeleg	שֶׁלֶג (ז)
it's snowing	yored 'ʃeleg	יוֹרֵד שֶׁלֶג
frost (severe ~, freezing cold)	kfor	כּפוֹר (ז)
below zero (adv)	mi'taχat la''efes	מִתַחַת לָאֶפֶס
hoarfrost	kfor	כּפוֹר (ז)
bad weather	sagrir	סַגרִיר (ז)
disaster	ason	אָסוֹן (ז)
flood, inundation	ʃitafon	שִׁיטָפוֹן (ז)
avalanche	ma'polet ʃlagim	מַפּוֹלֶת שׁלָגִים (נ)
earthquake	re'idat adama	רְעִידַת אֲדָמָה (נ)
tremor, quake	re'ida	רְעִידָה (נ)
epicenter	moked	מוֹקֵד (ז)
eruption	hitparʦut	הִתפָּרצוּת (נ)
lava	'lava	לָאבָה (נ)
tornado	tor'nado	טוֹרנָדוֹ (ז)
twister	hurikan	הוּרִיקָן (ז)
hurricane	hurikan	הוּרִיקָן (ז)
tsunami	ʦu'nami	צוּנָאמִי (ז)
cyclone	ʦiklon	צִיקלוֹן (ז)

22. Animals. Part 1

animal	'ba'al χayim	בַּעַל חַיִים (ז)
predator	χayat 'teref	חַיַת טֶרֶף (נ)
tiger	'tigris	טִיגרִיס (ז)
lion	arye	אַריֵה (ז)
wolf	ze'ev	זְאֵב (ז)
fox	ʃu'al	שׁוּעָל (ז)
jaguar	yagu'ar	יָגוּאָר (ז)
lynx	ʃunar	שׁוּנָר (ז)
coyote	ze'ev ha'aravot	זְאֵב הָעֲרָבוֹת (ז)
jackal	tan	תַן (ז)
hyena	ʦa'vo'a	צָבוֹעַ (ז)
squirrel	sna'i	סנָאִי (ז)
hedgehog	kipod	קִיפּוֹד (ז)
rabbit	ʃafan	שָׁפָן (ז)
raccoon	dvivon	דבִיבוֹן (ז)
hamster	oger	אוֹגֵר (ז)
mole	χafar'peret	חֲפַרפֶּרֶת (נ)
mouse	aχbar	עַכבָּר (ז)
rat	χulda	חוּלדָה (נ)
bat	atalef	עֲטַלֵף (ז)

beaver	bone	בּוֹנֶה (ז)
horse	sus	סוּס (ז)
deer	ayal	אַיָּל (ז)
camel	gamal	גָּמָל (ז)
zebra	'zebra	זֶּבּרָה (נ)

whale	livyatan	לְוויָתָן (ז)
seal	'kelev yam	כֶּלֶב יָם (ז)
walrus	sus yam	סוּס יָם (ז)
dolphin	dolfin	דוֹלפִין (ז)

bear	dov	דוֹב (ז)
monkey	kof	קוֹף (ז)
elephant	pil	פִּיל (ז)
rhinoceros	karnaf	קַרנַף (ז)
giraffe	dʒi'rafa	ג׳ירָפָה (נ)

hippopotamus	hipopotam	הִיפּוֹפּוֹטָם (ז)
kangaroo	'kenguru	קַנגוּרוּ (ז)
cat	xatula	חֲתוּלָה (נ)
dog	'kelev	כֶּלֶב (ז)

cow	para	פָּרָה (נ)
bull	ʃor	שׁוֹר (ז)
sheep (ewe)	kivsa	כִּבשָׂה (נ)
goat	ez	עֵז (נ)

donkey	xamor	חֲמוֹר (ז)
pig, hog	xazir	חֲזִיר (ז)
hen (chicken)	tarne'golet	תַרנְגוֹלֶת (נ)
rooster	tarnegol	תַרנְגוֹל (ז)

duck	barvaz	בַּרווָז (ז)
goose	avaz	אֲווָז (ז)
turkey (hen)	tarne'golet 'hodu	תַרנְגוֹלֶת הוֹדוּ (נ)
sheepdog	'kelev ro'e	כֶּלֶב רוֹעֶה (ז)

23. Animals. Part 2

bird	tsipor	צִיפּוֹר (נ)
pigeon	yona	יוֹנָה (נ)
sparrow	dror	דְרוֹר (ז)
tit (great tit)	yargazi	יַרגָזִי (ז)
magpie	orev nexalim	עוֹרֵב נְחָלִים (ז)

eagle	'ayit	עַיִט (ז)
hawk	nets	נֵץ (ז)
falcon	baz	בַּז (ז)
swan	barbur	בַּרבּוּר (ז)
crane	agur	עָגוּר (ז)

stork	χasida	חֲסִידָה (נ)
parrot	'tuki	תּוּכִּי (ז)
peacock	tavas	טַוָּוס (ז)
ostrich	bat ya'ana	בַּת יַעֲנָה (נ)
heron	anafa	אֲנָפָה (נ)
nightingale	zamir	זָמִיר (ז)
swallow	snunit	סְנוּנִית (נ)
woodpecker	'neker	נֶקֶר (ז)
cuckoo	kukiya	קוּקִיָּה (נ)
owl	yanʃuf	יַנְשׁוּף (ז)
penguin	pingvin	פִּינְגְּווִין (ז)
tuna	'tuna	טוּנָה (נ)
trout	forel	פוֹרֶל (ז)
eel	tslofaχ	צְלוֹפָח (ז)
shark	kariʃ	כָּרִישׁ (ז)
crab	sartan	סַרְטָן (ז)
jellyfish	me'duza	מֶדוּזָה (נ)
octopus	tamnun	תַּמְנוּן (ז)
starfish	koχav yam	כּוֹכַב יָם (ז)
sea urchin	kipod yam	קִיפּוֹד יָם (ז)
seahorse	suson yam	סוּסוֹן יָם (ז)
shrimp	χasilon	חֲסִילוֹן (ז)
snake	naχaʃ	נָחָשׁ (ז)
viper	'tsefa	צֶפַע (ז)
lizard	leta'a	לְטָאָה (נ)
iguana	igu"ana	אִיגוּאָנָה (נ)
chameleon	zikit	זִיקִית (נ)
scorpion	akrav	עַקְרָב (ז)
turtle	tsav	צָב (ז)
frog	tsfar'de'a	צְפַרְדֵּעַ (נ)
crocodile	tanin	תַּנִּין (ז)
insect, bug	χarak	חָרָק (ז)
butterfly	parpar	פַּרְפַּר (ז)
ant	nemala	נְמָלָה (נ)
fly	zvuv	זְבוּב (ז)
mosquito	yatuʃ	יַתּוּשׁ (ז)
beetle	χipuʃit	חִיפּוּשִׁית (נ)
bee	dvora	דְּבוֹרָה (נ)
spider	akaviʃ	עַכָּבִישׁ (ז)

24. Trees. Plants

tree	ets	עֵץ (ז)
birch	ʃadar	שָׁדָר (ז)

oak	alon	אַלוֹן (ז)
linden tree	'tilya	טִילְיָה (נ)
aspen	aspa	אַסְפָּה (נ)
maple	'eder	אֶדֶר (ז)
spruce	a'ʃuaχ	אַשּׁוּחַ (ז)
pine	'oren	אוֹרֶן (ז)
cedar	'erez	אֶרֶז (ז)
poplar	tsaftsefa	צַפְצָפָה (נ)
rowan	ben χuzrar	בֶּן־חוּזְרָר (ז)
beech	aʃur	אָשׁוּר (ז)
elm	bu'kitsa	בּוּקִיצָה (נ)
ash (tree)	mela	מֵילָה (נ)
chestnut	armon	עַרְמוֹן (ז)
palm tree	'dekel	דֶּקֶל (ז)
bush	'siaχ	שִׂיחַ (ז)
mushroom	pitriya	פִּטְרִיָּה (נ)
poisonous mushroom	pitriya ra'ila	פִּטְרִיָּה רַעֲלָה (נ)
cep (Boletus edulis)	por'tʃini	פּוֹרְצִ׳ינִי (ז)
russula	χarifit	חֲרִיפִית (נ)
fly agaric	zvuvanit	זְבוּבָנִית (נ)
death cap	pitriya ra'ila	פִּטְרִיָּה רַעֲלָה (נ)
flower	'peraχ	פֶּרַח (ז)
bouquet (of flowers)	zer	זֵר (ז)
rose (flower)	'vered	וֶרֶד (ז)
tulip	tsiv'oni	צִבְעוֹנִי (ז)
carnation	tsi'poren	צִיפּוֹרֶן (ז)
camomile	kamomil	קָמוֹמִיל (ז)
cactus	'kaktus	קַקְטוּס (ז)
lily of the valley	zivanit	זִיוָנִית (נ)
snowdrop	ga'lantus	גָּלַנְטוּס (ז)
water lily	nufar	נוּפָר (ז)
greenhouse (tropical ~)	χamama	חֲמָמָה (נ)
lawn	midʃa'a	מִדְשָׁאָה (נ)
flowerbed	arugat praχim	עֲרוּגַת פְּרָחִים (נ)
plant	'tsemaχ	צֶמַח (ז)
grass	'deʃe	דֶּשֶׁא (ז)
leaf	ale	עָלֶה (ז)
petal	ale ko'teret	עָלֶה כּוֹתֶרֶת (ז)
stem	giv'ol	גִּבְעוֹל (ז)
young plant (shoot)	'nevet	נֶבֶט (ז)
cereal crops	dganim	דְּגָנִים (ז״ר)
wheat	χita	חִיטָּה (נ)
rye	ʃifon	שִׁיפוֹן (ז)

oats	ʃi'bolet ʃu'al	שִׁיבּוֹלֶת שׁוּעָל (נ)
millet	'doχan	דּוֹחַן (ז)
barley	se'ora	שְׂעוֹרָה (נ)
corn	'tiras	תִּירָס (ז)
rice	'orez	אוֹרֶז (ז)

25. Various useful words

balance (of situation)	izun	אִיזוּן (ז)
base (basis)	basis	בָּסִיס (ז)
beginning	hatχala	הַתְחָלָה (נ)
category	kate'gorya	קָטֶגוֹרְיָה (נ)
choice	bχina	בְּחִינָה (נ)
coincidence	hat'ama	הַתְאָמָה (נ)
comparison	haʃva'a	הַשׁוְואָאָה (נ)
degree (extent, amount)	darga	דַּרְגָּה (נ)
development	hitpatχut	הִתְפַּתְחוּת (נ)
difference	'ʃoni	שׁוֹנִי (ז)
effect (e.g., of drugs)	efekt	אֶפֶקְט (ז)
effort (exertion)	ma'amats	מַאֲמָץ (ז)
element	element	אֶלֶמֶנְט (ז)
example (illustration)	dugma	דוּגְמָה (נ)
fact	uvda	עוּבְדָה (נ)
help	ezra	עֶזְרָה (נ)
ideal	ide'al	אִידֵיאָל (ז)
kind (sort, type)	sug	סוּג (ז)
mistake, error	ta'ut	טָעוּת (נ)
moment	'rega	רֶגַע (ז)
obstacle	maχsom	מַחְסוֹם (ז)
part (~ of sth)	'χelek	חֵלֶק (ז)
pause (break)	hafuga	הֲפוּגָה (נ)
position	emda	עֶמְדָה (נ)
problem	be'aya	בְּעָיָה (נ)
process	tahaliχ	תַּהֲלִיךְ (ז)
progress	kidma	קִדְמָה (נ)
property (quality)	tχuna, sgula	תכוּנָה, סְגוּלָה (נ)
reaction	tguva	תְגוּבָה (נ)
risk	sikun	סִיכּוּן (ז)
secret	sod	סוֹד (ז)
series	sidra	סִדְרָה (נ)
shape (outer form)	tsura	צוּרָה (נ)
situation	matsav	מַצָּב (ז)

solution	pitaron	פִּיתָרוֹן (ז)
standard (adj)	tikni	תִקְנִי
stop (pause)	hafsaka	הַפְסָקָה (נ)
style	signon	סִגְנוֹן (ז)
system	ſita	שִׁיטָה (נ)
table (chart)	tavla	טַבְלָה (נ)
tempo, rate	'ketsev	קֶצֶב (ז)
term (word, expression)	musag	מוּשָׂג (ז)
truth (e.g., moment of ~)	emet	אֱמֶת (נ)
turn (please wait your ~)	tor	תוֹר (ז)
urgent (adj)	daχuf	דָחוּף
utility (usefulness)	to''elet	תוֹעֶלֶת (נ)
variant (alternative)	girsa	גִירסָה (נ)
way (means, method)	'ofen	אוֹפֶן (ז)
zone	ezor	אֵזוֹר (ז)

26. Modifiers. Adjectives. Part 1

additional (adj)	nosaf	נוֹסָף
ancient (~ civilization)	atik	עָתִיק
artificial (adj)	melaχuti	מְלָאכוּתִי
bad (adj)	ra	רַע
beautiful (person)	yafe	יָפֶה
big (in size)	gadol	גָדוֹל
bitter (taste)	marir	מָרִיר
blind (sightless)	iver	עִיוֵר
central (adj)	merkazi	מֶרכָּזִי
children's (adj)	yaldi	יַלדִי
clandestine (secret)	maχtarti	מַחתַרתִי
clean (free from dirt)	naki	נָקִי
clever (smart)	pi'keaχ	פִּיקֵחַ
compatible (adj)	to'em	תוֹאֵם
contented (satisfied)	merutse	מְרוּצֶה
dangerous (adj)	mesukan	מְסוּכָּן
dead (not alive)	met	מֵת
dense (fog, smoke)	tsafuf	צָפוּף
difficult (decision)	kaſe	קָשֶׁה
dirty (not clean)	meluχlaχ	מְלוּכלָך
easy (not difficult)	kal	קַל
empty (glass, room)	rek	רֵיק
exact (amount)	meduyak	מְדוּיָק
excellent (adj)	metsuyan	מְצוּיָן
excessive (adj)	meyutar	מְיוּתָר

exterior (adj)	xitsoni	חִיצוֹנִי
fast (quick)	mahir	מָהִיר
fertile (land, soil)	pore	פּוֹרֶה
fragile (china, glass)	ʃavir	שָׁבִיר

free (at no cost)	xinam	חִינָם
fresh (~ water)	metukim	מְתוּקִים
frozen (food)	kafu	קָפוּא
full (completely filled)	male	מָלֵא
happy (adj)	me'uʃar	מְאוּשָׁר

hard (not soft)	kaʃe	קָשֶׁה
huge (adj)	anaki	עֲנָקִי
ill (sick, unwell)	xole	חוֹלֶה
immobile (adj)	xasar tnu'a	חֲסַר תְּנוּעָה
important (adj)	xaʃuv	חָשׁוּב

interior (adj)	pnimi	פְּנִימִי
last (e.g., ~ week)	ʃe'avar	שֶׁעָבַר
last (final)	axaron	אַחֲרוֹן
left (e.g., ~ side)	smali	שְׂמָאלִי
legal (legitimate)	xuki	חוּקִי

light (in weight)	kal	קַל
liquid (fluid)	nozli	נוֹזְלִי
long (e.g., ~ hair)	arox	אָרוֹךְ
loud (voice, etc.)	ram	רָם
low (voice)	ʃaket	שָׁקֵט

27. Modifiers. Adjectives. Part 2

main (principal)	raʃi	רָאשִׁי
matt, matte	mat	מַט
mysterious (adj)	mistori	מִסְתּוֹרִי
narrow (street, etc.)	tsar	צַר
native (~ country)	ʃel mo'ledet	שֶׁל מוֹלֶדֶת

negative (~ response)	ʃlili	שְׁלִילִי
new (adj)	xadaʃ	חָדָשׁ
next (e.g., ~ week)	haba	הַבָּא
normal (adj)	nor'mali	נוֹרְמָלִי
not difficult (adj)	lo kaʃe	לֹא קָשֶׁה

obligatory (adj)	hexrexi	חֶכְרֵחִי
old (house)	yaʃan	יָשָׁן
open (adj)	pa'tuax	פָּתוֹחַ
opposite (adj)	negdi	נֶגְדִּי
ordinary (usual)	ragil	רָגִיל
original (unusual)	mekori	מְקוֹרִי
personal (adj)	prati	פְּרָטִי

| polite (adj) | menumas | מְנוּמָס |
| poor (not rich) | ani | עָנִי |

possible (adj)	efʃari	אֶפְשָׁרִי
principal (main)	ikari	עִיקָרִי
probable (adj)	efʃari	אֶפְשָׁרִי
prolonged (e.g., ~ applause)	memuʃax	מְמוּשָׁךְ
public (open to all)	tsiburi	צִיבּוּרִי

rare (adj)	nadir	נָדִיר
raw (uncooked)	xai	חַי
right (not left)	yemani	יְמָנִי
ripe (fruit)	baʃel	בָּשֵׁל

risky (adj)	mesukan	מְסוּכָּן
sad (~ look)	atsuv	עָצוּב
second hand (adj)	meʃumaʃ	מְשׁוּמָשׁ
shallow (water)	radud	רָדוּד
sharp (blade, etc.)	xad	חַד

short (in length)	katsar	קָצָר
similar (adj)	dome	דוֹמֶה
small (in size)	katan	קָטָן
smooth (surface)	xalak	חָלָק
soft (~ toys)	rax	רַךְ

solid (~ wall)	mutsak	מוּצָק
sour (flavor, taste)	xamuts	חָמוּץ
spacious (house, etc.)	meruvax	מְרוּוָח
special (adj)	meyuxad	מְיוּחָד

straight (line, road)	yaʃar	יָשָׁר
strong (person)	xazak	חָזָק
stupid (foolish)	tipeʃ	טִיפֵּשׁ
superb, perfect (adj)	metsuyan	מְצוּיָן

sweet (sugary)	matok	מָתוֹק
tan (adj)	ʃazuf	שָׁזוּף
tasty (delicious)	ta'im	טָעִים
unclear (adj)	lo barur	לֹא בָּרוּר

28. Verbs. Part 1

to accuse (vt)	leha'aʃim	לְהַאֲשִׁים
to agree (say yes)	lehaskim	לְהַסְכִּים
to announce (vt)	leho'dia	לְהוֹדִיעַ
to answer (vi, vt)	la'anot	לַעֲנוֹת
to apologize (vi)	lehitnatsel	לְהִתְנַצֵּל
to arrive (vi)	leha'gi'a	לְהַגִּיעַ

to ask (~ oneself)	liʃ'ol	לִשְׁאוֹל
to be absent	lehe'ader	לְהֵיעָדֵר
to be afraid	lefaχed	לְפַחֵד
to be born	lehivaled	לְהִיוָּלֵד

to be in a hurry	lemaher	לְמַהֵר
to beat (to hit)	lehakot	לְהַכּוֹת
to begin (vt)	lehatχil	לְהַתְחִיל
to believe (in God)	leha'amin	לְהַאֲמִין
to belong to …	lehiʃtayeχ	לְהִשְׁתַּיֵּיךְ
to break (split into pieces)	liʃbor	לִשְׁבּוֹר

to build (vt)	livnot	לִבְנוֹת
to buy (purchase)	liknot	לִקְנוֹת
can (v aux)	yaχol	יָכוֹל
can (v aux)	yaχol	יָכוֹל
to cancel (call off)	levatel	לְבַטֵּל

to catch (vt)	litfos	לִתְפּוֹס
to change (vt)	leʃanot	לְשַׁנּוֹת
to check (to examine)	livdok	לִבְדּוֹק
to choose (select)	livχor	לִבְחוֹר
to clean up (tidy)	lesader	לְסַדֵּר
to close (vt)	lisgor	לִסְגּוֹר
to compare (vt)	lehaʃvot	לְהַשְׁווֹת
to complain (vi, vt)	lehitlonen	לְהִתְלוֹנֵן
to confirm (vt)	le'aʃer	לְאַשֵּׁר
to congratulate (vt)	levareχ	לְבָרֵךְ

to cook (dinner)	levaʃel	לְבַשֵּׁל
to copy (vt)	leha'atik	לְהַעֲתִיק
to cost (vt)	la'alot	לַעֲלוֹת
to count (add up)	lispor	לִסְפּוֹר
to count on …	lismoχ al	לִסְמוֹךְ עַל

to create (vt)	litsor	לִיצוֹר
to cry (weep)	livkot	לִבְכּוֹת
to dance (vi, vt)	lirkod	לִרְקוֹד
to deceive (vi, vt)	leramot	לְרַמּוֹת
to decide (~ to do sth)	lehaχlit	לְהַחְלִיט

to delete (vt)	limχok	לִמְחוֹק
to demand (request firmly)	lidroʃ	לִדְרוֹשׁ
to deny (vt)	liʃlol	לִשְׁלוֹל
to depend on …	lihyot talui be…	לִהְיוֹת תָּלוּי בְּ…
to despise (vt)	lezalzel be…	לְזַלְזֵל בְּ…

to die (vi)	lamut	לָמוּת
to dig (vt)	laχpor	לַחְפּוֹר
to disappear (vi)	lehe'alem	לְהֵיעָלֵם
to discuss (vt)	ladun	לָדוּן
to disturb (vt)	lehafri'a	לְהַפְרִיעַ

29. Verbs. Part 2

to dive (vi)	liʦlol	לִצְלוֹל
to divorce (vi)	lehitgareʃ mi…	לְהִתְגָּרֵשׁ מ...
to do (vt)	la'asot	לַעֲשׂוֹת
to doubt (have doubts)	lefakpek	לְפַקְפֵּק
to drink (vi, vt)	liʃtot	לִשְׁתּוֹת
to drop (let fall)	lehapil	לְהַפִּיל
to dry (clothes, hair)	leyabeʃ	לְיַבֵּשׁ
to eat (vi, vt)	le'exol	לֶאֱכוֹל
to end (~ a relationship)	lesayem	לְסַיֵּם
to excuse (forgive)	lis'loax	לִסְלוֹחַ
to exist (vi)	lehitkayem	לְהִתְקַיֵּם
to expect (foresee)	laxazot	לַחֲזוֹת
to explain (vt)	lehasbir	לְהַסְבִּיר
to fall (vi)	lipol	לִיפּוֹל
to fight (street fight, etc.)	lehitkotet	לְהִתְקוֹטֵט
to find (vt)	limʦo	לִמְצוֹא
to finish (vt)	lesayem	לְסַיֵּם
to fly (vi)	la'uf	לָעוּף
to forbid (vt)	le'esor al	לֶאֱסוֹר עַל
to forget (vi, vt)	liʃ'koax	לִשְׁכּוֹחַ
to forgive (vt)	lis'loax	לִסְלוֹחַ
to get tired	lehit'ayef	לְהִתְעַיֵּיף
to give (vt)	latet	לָתֵת
to go (on foot)	la'lexet	לָלֶכֶת
to hate (vt)	lisno	לִשְׂנוֹא
to have (vt)	lehaxzik	לְהַחְזִיק
to have breakfast	le'exol aruxat 'boker	לֶאֱכוֹל אֲרוּחַת בּוֹקֶר
to have dinner	le'exol aruxat 'erev	לֶאֱכוֹל אֲרוּחַת עֶרֶב
to have lunch	le'exol aruxat ʦaha'rayim	לֶאֱכוֹל אֲרוּחַת צָהֳרַיִים
to hear (vt)	liʃ'mo'a	לִשְׁמוֹעַ
to help (vt)	la'azor	לַעֲזוֹר
to hide (vt)	lehastir	לְהַסְתִּיר
to hope (vi, vt)	lekavot	לְקַווֹת
to hunt (vi, vt)	laʦud	לָצוּד
to hurry (vi)	lemaher	לְמַהֵר
to insist (vi, vt)	lehit'akeʃ	לְהִתְעַקֵּשׁ
to insult (vt)	leha'aliv	לְהַעֲלִיב
to invite (vt)	lehazmin	לְהַזְמִין
to joke (vi)	lehitba'deax	לְהִתְבַּדֵּחַ
to keep (vt)	liʃmor	לִשְׁמוֹר
to kill (vt)	laharog	לַהֲרוֹג
to know (sb)	lehakir et	לְהַכִּיר אֶת

to know (sth)	la'da'at	לָדַעַת
to like (I like …)	limtso χen be'ei'nayim	לִמְצוֹא חֵן בְּעֵינַיִים
to look at …	lehistakel	לְהִסְתַּכֵּל
to lose (umbrella, etc.)	le'abed	לְאַבֵּד
to love (sb)	le'ehov	לֶאֱהוֹב
to make a mistake	lit'ot	לִטְעוֹת
to meet (vi, vt)	lehipageʃ	לְהִיפָּגֵשׁ
to miss (school, etc.)	lehaχsir	לְהַחְסִיר

30. Verbs. Part 3

to obey (vi, vt)	letsayet	לְצַיֵּת
to open (vt)	lif'toaχ	לִפְתּוֹחַ
to participate (vi)	lehiʃtatef	לְהִשְׁתַּתֵּף
to pay (vi, vt)	leʃalem	לְשַׁלֵּם
to permit (vt)	leharʃot	לְהַרְשׁוֹת
to play (children)	lesaχek	לְשַׂחֵק
to pray (vi, vt)	lehitpalel	לְהִתְפַּלֵּל
to promise (vt)	lehav'tiaχ	לְהַבְטִיחַ
to propose (vt)	leha'tsi'a	לְהַצִּיעַ
to prove (vt)	leho'χiaχ	לְהוֹכִיחַ
to read (vi, vt)	likro	לִקְרוֹא
to receive (vt)	lekabel	לְקַבֵּל
to rent (sth from sb)	liskor	לִשְׂכּוֹר
to repeat (say again)	laχazor al	לַחֲזוֹר עַל
to reserve, to book	lehazmin meroʃ	לְהַזְמִין מֵרֹאשׁ
to run (vi)	laruts	לָרוּץ
to save (rescue)	lehatsil	לְהַצִּיל
to say (~ thank you)	lomar	לוֹמַר
to see (vt)	lir'ot	לִרְאוֹת
to sell (vt)	limkor	לִמְכּוֹר
to send (vt)	liʃ'loaχ	לִשְׁלוֹחַ
to shoot (vi)	lirot	לִירוֹת
to shout (vi)	lits'ok	לִצְעוֹק
to show (vt)	lehar'ot	לְהַרְאוֹת
to sign (document)	laχtom	לַחְתּוֹם
to sing (vi)	laʃir	לָשִׁיר
to sit down (vi)	lehityaʃev	לְהִתְיַישֵׁב
to smile (vi)	leχayeχ	לְחַיֵּיךְ
to speak (vi, vt)	ledaber	לְדַבֵּר
to steal (money, etc.)	lignov	לִגְנוֹב
to stop (please ~ calling me)	lehafsik	לְהַפְסִיק
to study (vt)	lilmod	לִלְמוֹד

to swim (vi)	lisχot	לִשְׂחוֹת
to take (vt)	la'kaχat	לָקַחַת
to talk to ...	ledaber	לְדַבֵּר
to tell (story, joke)	lesaper	לְסַפֵּר
to thank (vt)	lehodot	לְהוֹדוֹת
to think (vi, vt)	laχʃov	לַחְשׁוֹב
to translate (vt)	letargem	לְתַרְגֵם
to trust (vt)	liv'toaχ	לִבְטוֹחַ
to try (attempt)	lenasot	לְנַסּוֹת
to turn (e.g., ~ left)	lifnot	לִפְנוֹת
to turn off	leχabot	לְכַבּוֹת
to turn on	lehadlik	לְהַדְלִיק
to understand (vt)	lehavin	לְהָבִין
to wait (vt)	lehamtin	לְהַמְתִּין
to want (wish, desire)	lirtsot	לִרְצוֹת
to work (vi)	la'avod	לַעֲבוֹד
to write (vt)	liχtov	לִכְתּוֹב